BRITISH RAILWAYS ILLUSTRATED

ANNUAL 14

Welcome to British Railways II

ILLUSTRATED

...trated ANNUAL 14

All New Photographs and Articles!

Cover: **Bournemouth Central in the early 1960s, and Merchant Navy Pacific 35024 EAST ASIATIC COMPANY. Paul Hocquard, The Transport Treasury.**

Rear cover: **Haymarket A1 60152 HOLYROOD leaves Edinburgh Waverley. George Heiron, courtesy Mrs Shirley Heiron, The Transport Treasury.**

Frontispiece: **Grangemouth close-up, 1964. Paul Hocquard, The Transport Treasury.**

EDITORIAL MATTERS
Contributions,
submissions, photographs or whatever
(remember the contributor must
address and attend to
copyright), readers'
letters, bouquets
and brickbats for
British Railways Illustrated
must be addressed to Editor,
Chris Hawkins
at 59A, High Street, Clophill,
Bedfordshire MK45 4BE
E-mail chris@irwellpress.co.uk
Tel.01525 861888 or
Fax. 01525 862044
Printed & Bound by
Newton Printing
Copyright :- Irwell Press Ltd. 2005

You'll Remember those Black and White Days...

.IRWELLPRESS.CO.UK E-mail George@Irwellpress.co.uk

IRWELL PRESS
No.1 in Railway Publishing

Express Exchanges

Notes by Tony Wright, Assistant Editor British Railway Modelling magazine

The 'Big Four' independent railway companies in this realm ceased to exist by act of Parliament at midnight on December 31 1947, thus becoming the nationalised British Railways. Enthusiasts' interest was heightened when, starting in the spring of the following year, there was a series of locomotive exchanges, where individual locos of the separate companies 'competed' against each other over the main lines. There were three different categories, these being express passenger, mixed traffic and freight. Locos in the express listings were GWR 'King', Southern 'Merchant Navy', LMS rebuilt 'Royal Scot', LMS 'Princess Coronation' and LNER A4. Locos in the mixed traffic group were GWR 'Hall', Southern 'West Country', LMS 'Black Five' and LNER B1. Locos in the freight group were GWR 38XX, LMS 8F, LNER O1 and 'Austerity' 2-8-0 and 2-10-0. The Southern, having no heavy freight loco, had no part to play in this. Some types, the likes of which one might consider suitable for inclusion, were precluded because of restrictions, thus the modern GWR 'County' 4-6-0 and the truly

mixed traffic V2 2-6-2 took no part. There was no passenger tank loco category of any kind, nor shunting group. Surely, too, some form of 'competition' between the tender 0-6-0s might also have been arranged? Imagine the effect on the dead-handed Anderson's reputation there would be if the 4Fs had been pitted against the Q1s! Ah, daydreams.

In truth, unless in the unlikely event of one particular class being so superior to the others in its category, nothing would really change, especially as old allegiances (even for pre-Group practice) were still firmly intact. Indeed for several years afterwards locos of pre-Nationalisation design continued to be built. The 'Royal Scot' placed amongst the 'big boys' seems a trifle unfair, though it acquitted itself well. Placing the powerful 'West Country' Pacifics amongst much smaller 'competitors' also seems unfair, and it certainly outperformed them in every respect, including much higher coal consumption. However, such was its 'revolutionary' design that it had no hope of ever being adopted as standard, even though it 'blew the

opposition away' in terms of power output. In the event, the Locomotive Committee of the new BR was formed of ex-LMS men, with Riddles as 'gaffer'. In fairness, though most of the subsequent BR Standard classes had an almost exact ex-LMS equivalent (and perhaps, therefore should not have been built) many of the detail features came from elsewhere, and at least the design work was spread across the other 'railway' towns as well as Crewe. As it was, the best (and the worst) of the Standards were entirely new designs, having no pre-Nationalisation equivalent, so it could be argued that the exchanges were a waste of time and money. Certainly to what degree the excellence of the 'Britannias' or 9Fs was owed to the spring of 1948 is a moot point. The 'Clans' weren't needed anyway and 71000 only came into existence because of the destruction of PRINCESS ANNE at Harrow though, by all accounts now built 'properly', she has the beating of all the other 8Ps in the exchanges. Anyway, who could have predicted at the start of that wonderfully optimistic time that in just twenty years, steam would be

Class A4 60033 SEAGULL on the 1.30pm express from Paddington to Plymouth (the designated Down WR train for the tests – the return working was the 8.30am from Plymouth next day) on April 24 1948. Presumably this was one of the trial runs before the tests proper, for a dynamometer car is not attached. The loco still has its LNER garter blue livery, though by this time lettered BRITISH RAILWAYS and with 60,000 added to its final LNER number. The allocation, Kings+, is painted on the front of the casing (BR cast shed plates came later) and the front numberplate has been installed on the wedge front. The '6' is incorrect, though, having a curly tail – not correct Gill sans. This was never corrected. Photograph J.C. Flemons, The Transport Treasury.

The A4s

banished from BR? I doubt if the pioneer LMS or SR main line diesels were even considered as participants in the exchanges, such was the long-term perception of steam's future at the time.

Isn't it wonderful to speculate on a further set of regional exchanges a decade later with diesels included, or another set exclusively diesel? The prospect of double-chimney 'Kings', rebuilt 'Merchant Navys', Stanier Pacifics, A1s and A4s beating the daylights out of EE Type 4s and 'Warships' is something to savour. Perhaps a series of comparative tests should have taken place among the early BR diesels. That way the hopeless duplication and proliferation of 'dud' types across the whole power range might have been partially avoided. As it was, enthusiasts will have to speculate forever as to which would 'win' between a 'Western' or a 'Deltic' (no prizes for guessing my choice!), an EE Type 3, 'Hymek' or Birmingham RC&W Type 3 or an EE Type 4 and a 'Peak'.

Today, nearly 60 years after the event, what about an exchange between the likes of 91s, 'Eurostars'

and 'Pendolinos', or the various types of diesel units? At least the proceedings would be polychromatic in the extreme and photographed thus.

The photographs are by J.C. Flemons, whose work is familiar in the pages of British Railways Illustrated. *He obviously set out to record the passenger engines but was restricted to London and its NW hinterland (he lived at Pinner) and either had no interest in the freight locos or, more likely, was not privy to the workings – or those workings, maybe, took place at inconvenient times.*

SEAGULL near Ealing, with the 8.30am Plymouth-Paddington on May 5 1948. The WR dynamometer car is attached, suggesting this is one of the actual test trains. 60033 certainly impressed the running department of the former GWR during the trials, so much so that, after this great bird had arrived at Paddington a WR Locomotive Inspector (as reported in the revered RCTS 'Green Guide') declared: 'We have nothing to touch this engine'. The results of the 1925 exchanges reversed? Photograph J.C. Flemons, The Transport Treasury.

Bushey troughs is the unmistakable location as 60034 LORD FARINGDON heads the 10.00 am Down 'Royal Scot' on May 17 1948. No dynamometer car is present so it's one of the trial runs, though it's the 'official' test train which the loco will take as far as Carlisle, a typical 'Semi' diagram of the day (or any day up to the early 1960s). The consist appears to be typical Stanier 'Period 3' stock. 'Porthole' stock would be making its appearance about this time (though clear LMS in design, much of it was built after Nationalisation). Photograph J.C. Flemons, The Transport Treasury.

A wonderful picture taken on a glorious May 27 1948, as LORD FARINGDON heads north over Bushey troughs at 10.24am on the Down 'Royal Scot', the consist including the LMS dynamometer car as the first vehicle. Like SEAGULL, she now carries her BR front numberplate, but this has only recently been fitted. Prior to the runs on 'foreign' metals, 60034 was tested on her home road, but with her BR number (in incorrect curly- tailed Gill sans) just painted on the casing between her left-hand buffer and coupling. Presumably, after the number was painted out there wasn't time to paint in her home shed. The cast front numberplate now fitted has, like sister SEAGULL, the incorrect 6, but this will eventually be corrected, though much later in her life, post-1963. Curious, isn't it, how money could be 'wasted' on a loco nearing the end of its days? During the earlier tests, from April 20-23 inclusive, the dynamometer car was attached at the front of the regular passenger turn between Kings Cross and Leeds return. Apparently, on one or two of the days, there were complaints in the train about how cold it was, for the set (it was an English spring after all) was not pre-heated. The loco then had to provide steam heating as well as power the train, and when this was taken into consideration, the economy figures for the A4 were even better. Photograph J.C. Flemons, The Transport Treasury.

On the last day of May 1948, SEAGULL heads west approaching Vauxhall on the 10.50am express to the West Country, formed of the latest Bulleid stock of the day. As such she appears typical of an A4 of the period (other than being one of the minority with double pots and having one of the trio of cut-down corridor tenders) with full width dust shield, superfluous frame-mounted guard irons and extended cylinder drain cock pipes. The two SR discs tell any signalman that she's heading on the ex-LSWR route to the far west (the Southern identified their trains by destination, Up and Down, rather than status) providing at least two more brackets than the others. Were these trials on the SR the only time that the A4s ran without headlamps? Whilst the other members of the 'Big Four' submitted their latest Class 7 (later class 8) motive power for the tests (other than the ex-LMS rebuilt 'Scot'), this was not so for the Eastern.

Thompson's A2/3s were only one/two years old and his A1/1 just three. Had Thompson still been in charge as ER CME he might well have leant on the operating department to submit one of his locos for the test. Peppercorn's A2s were brand new, but even with him at the helm (his A1s were still a season away) the A4s it was. Anyway, such was the anti-Thompson feeling among many of his former officers at the time, it's inconceivable that any of his Pacifics would have been considered. Photograph J.C. Flemons, The Transport Treasury.

The most celebrated A4 of all, no less than the world speed record holder herself, No.22 MALLARD, heads the 10.50am Waterloo-Exeter near Vauxhall on June 6 1948. MALLARD, being so famous, was an obvious ER choice for the trials but there is evidence that the 'blokes in the know' were not happy with No.22's selection. Clearly those A4s fitted with double Kylchap chimneys were definite choices (there were just four of them – why, when it was known before the war how much better the quartet performed, did it take a further two decades before all the class had this free-steaming feature?) but MALLARD wasn't in the best of fettle at the time. Early in 1948 she'd been the last A4 to retain wartime black, when she was repainted in garter blue. One assumes an overhaul was undertaken at the same time, which should have meant she was nicely run-in by the spring (one of the conditions of the tests was that the locos should have run 15,000-20,000 miles since overhaul) but she didn't shine. On one occasion she failed on the Southern and had to be replaced by SEAGULL. However, she certainly looked good, if a little of a hybrid with stainless steel numbers (prefixed by a non-stainless steel 'E') and BRITISH RAILWAYS painted on her tender. The plaques, a post-war addition commemorating the record run, are proudly displayed on her flanks. When she was preserved in 1963 and returned to her record-breaking condition (getting back a streamlined non-corridor tender) the plaques were retained. So, strictly speaking, her appearance was not dead right for July 3, 1938. Some eminent railway (and model railway) correspondents suggested that her badges of achievement should have been taken off, for 'absolute' accuracy of course. What utter nonsense! Fortunately, enough people with common sense made the right decision and the pedants were silenced. Photograph J.C. Flemons, The Transport Treasury.

46236 CITY OF BRADFORD approaches Finsbury Park on the 7.50am ex-Leeds express at 12.12pm on April 29 1948. The loco sports the handsome 1946 straw-lined black LMS livery, but with British Railways lettering and numbering. The '4' prefixing 6236 can be seen shoehorned in on the front numberplate, for it's a bit bigger than the rest of the cast numerals. Evidence of the loco's former streamlined status is clear from the sloping smokebox top, thus identifying this 'Princess Coronation/Duchess' as a 'Semi'. Whether this epithet was supposed to imply semi-streamlined I don't know, though it hardly seems appropriate. To us 'urchin' trainspotters at Chester, every Stanier 'big-un' was a 'Semi', just as every 'Black Five' was a 'Mickey', except the Caprotti versions which rejoiced in the name 'Gorillas', presumably because of their pronounced outside steam pipes. The rivalry between the LMS and LNER adherents meant that the 'contest' between the A4s and the 'Semi' was keenly followed. Without doubt, the latter was the more reliable (46236 was the only one used over all the routes) but the A4s were the more economical and equalled the bigger loco in terms of power output. Some question the way the 'Duchess' was driven (all the locos in the exchanges had their own crews, with conductors on 'foreign' routes as necessary) where the driver might have been over-cautious perhaps. Cecil J. Allen considered the contest 'honours easy'. Who knows? The next time a 'big-un' worked over the ex-GN main line was in the summer of 1963, when CITY OF LONDON took a special to Doncaster and back. Photograph J.C. Flemons, The Transport Treasury.

CITY OF BRADFORD, now on the Western with dynamometer car in tow, passing Old Oak Lane on May 20, 1948. Note how the sloping smokebox imparts an odd look to the chimney. Photograph J.C. Flemons, The Transport Treasury.

The sole representative of the ex-LMS 'Princess Coronation' Pacifics used in the exchanges, 46236 CITY OF BRADFORD, at Vauxhall heading (according to David Jenkinson) the 'Atlantic Coast Express', the 10.50am Waterloo-Exeter on June 22 1948. The ex-GWR dynamometer car is the first vehicle, just behind the distinctive 'Austerity' eight-wheeled tender lettered LMS – someone had a sense of mischief. This was substituted to ensure sufficient water, there being no troughs anywhere on the Southern. The 'Semi's' own tender's capacity was deemed insufficient for the 90-plus miles it might be expected to run without replenishment. The A4s had no problem because of their bigger tenders, like the indigenous Bulleid Pacifics. The 'King' involved in the tests was barred from the ex-LSWR route, so the spectacle of a GWR 4-6-0 with an 'Austerity' tender never materialised. Photograph J.C. Flemons, The Transport Treasury.

The King

The Western representative in the 'big stuff' category, 6018 KING HENRY VI approaches Wood Green, heading the 7.50am express ex-Leeds on May 13 1948. The GW ATC was removed for the duration of the tests, though the front coupling, in true GWR style, is hooked up out of the way to prevent damage to the shoe. In truth, the ex-GWR men can't have expected too much of these exchanges. Their loco had an axle loading that was too heavy, was out of loading gauge for most lines (including many on its own system) and was 20 years old, nothing more modern of similar power having since been built at Swindon. Partisans will argue nothing was needed but an express loco design with inside valve gear wasn't going to set any pace post-war. At least the coal supplied was appropriate Welsh steam, but a 'fussy eater' was never going to be tolerated in a period of austerity. However, and this must not be forgotten, when the 'Kings' got double chimneys in the 1950s, the now 30-year old veterans easily achieved the new 'accelerated' diesel schedules – they had to as the hopeless A-1-A 'Warships' weren't reliable enough and the lighter 'Warships' not powerful enough. It was only after the 'Westerns' appeared that the 'Kings' were finally dethroned. Photograph J.C. Flemons, The Transport Treasury.

The 'King' attacks the climb towards Potters Bar on one of the test trains, the 1.10pm from Kings Cross complete with the ex-LNER dynamometer car, 18 May 1948. Like the sole 'Duchess', 6018 KING HENRY VI showed great reliability and tackled whatever job was given with relative ease. This site today is unrecognisable with four tracks and overhead catenary everywhere. Photograph J.C. Flemons, The Transport Treasury.

The Merchant Navys

A gaggle of spectators at Paddington await with great interest the departure of 35019 FRENCH LINE CGT to Plymouth on 19 May 1948. The loco is one of the later series with improved look-out 'V' cab and is coupled to a black-painted ex-LMS tender in order to be able to pick up water en-route. Pre-nationalisation insignia were supposed to be expunged and like the 'LMS' on the WD tender behind 46236 CITY OF BRADFORD on the Southern Region the retention of the SOUTHERN smokebox door roundel was surely not accidental. Photograph J.C. Flemons, The Transport Treasury.

35019 FRENCH LINE CGT seems to be in fine fettle as she heads away from the capital near Acton on the WR, April 21 1948. Two 'Merchant Navys' took part in the 'away' exchanges – a third, BIBBY LINE, had an LMS tender attached but in the event was not needed. 35018 BRITISH INDIA LINE did the honours on the home ground's trials. With fewer complete loco failures, it could be said that the Doncaster-trained Bulleid's locos were more reliable than Gresley's, and as far as the exchanges go, this is true. Photograph J.C. Flemons, The Transport Treasury.

35017 BELGIAN MARINE near Kenton in the London outskirts with the 12.55 from Carlisle, running 35 minutes late on April 14 1948. Not too much should be made of the lateness because of all the routes selected, the ex-LNW main line had by far the most restrictions at the time, and the SR men were more likely than any of the others to attempt to make up lost time, however much coal was chucked in – and out! Photograph J.C. Flemons, The Transport Treasury.

The famous splitting signals at Greenwood form part of the location around 35019 FRENCH LINE CGT on May 18 1948 as she heads for Kings Cross at 11.58am in charge of the 7.50am ex-Leeds express. The crew is probably Driver G. James and Fireman G. Reynolds from Nine Elms shed. Photograph J.C. Flemons, The Transport Treasury.

35017 BELGIAN MARINE passing Potters Bar on the 1.10 Down express. Photograph J.C. Flemons, The Transport Treasury.

French's magnificent sky-background somersault signals indicate a clear road towards the 'Cross as 35017 BELGIAN MARINE passes Finsbury Park on May 26 1948. Although generally reliable throughout the exchanges, the 'Merchants' suffered from several niggling faults throughout the period. Given their revolutionary design, this is probably understandable. Photograph J.C. Flemons, The Transport Treasury.

'West Country' 34006 BUDE near Northwood, heading the 8.25am from Manchester London Road to Marylebone on June 1 1948. The train at this point is running on Metropolitan and Great Central Joint metals. As with their bigger sisters, the 'away' light Pacifics towed LMS tenders to enable them to pick up water en route. BUDE sports the extra large deflector plates fitted to a few of the class. Photograph J.C. Flemons, The Transport Treasury.

The West Countrys

In order to get the 'West Country' up to Scotland so that it could participate in the runs between Perth and Inverness a path had to be found, in this case by piloting the 5.05pm express ex-Euston as far as Crewe. From there the loco piloted a Perth express. Coming home, the loco took a heavy express from Perth to Carlisle unassisted over Beattock summit. The 'WC' in question is 34004 YEOVIL and she too has the longer deflector plates and LMS tender – the latter will be fitted with a tablet-exchange device for working over the single-track Highland main line when she gets to Perth. The third 'WC' selected, 34005 BARNSTAPLE was also fitted with an LMS tender. Of all the individual 'feats' achieved during the exchanges, YEOVIL's probably stands out the most when she accelerated the 4.00pm Perth-Inverness so rapidly up to Druimuachdar summit that she 'winded' the indigenous 4-4-0 to the extent that the train had to be stopped in order that the veteran could 'get its breath back'. Supporters of the Highland loco might claim that its discomfiture was because it had done more than its fair share of the work, but Bulleid's light Pacifics could take prodigious loads unassisted unless conditions were greasy when their propensity for slipping (which was never cured) restricted them. Driver J. Swain and his mate fireman A. Hooker were 'unofficially' told to not give a fig about coal consumption but show what their steed could do, the Southern being the smallest of the groups and, until the advent of Bulleids, rather second class when it came to 'the big stuff'. Photograph J.C. Flemons, The Transport Treasury.

The only participant in the Class 6 power range (later Class 7) was Royal Scot 4-6-0 46162 QUEEN'S WESTMINSTER RIFLEMAN. On April 19 1948 the engine is backing down to connect to the 1.10pm to Leeds at Kings Cross. Observe the various cables and conduit in place on the tender rear for connection to the dynamometer car. The livery is hybrid – LMS still on the tender, but with 40,000 added to the LMS number, the style of which is still pre-Nationalisation. This black/straw-lined post-war livery was very handsome and fully in the LNW tradition of no unnecessary frills. In time the 'Scot' will get smoke deflectors and BR green, but that's a bit in the future yet. Photograph J.C. Flemons, The Transport Treasury.

The ever-reliable rebuilt 'Scot' approaches Finsbury Park at 60 mph on April 30 heading one of the Up test trains – note the various cables running along the base of the tender tank, for the recording instruments in the dynamometer car. It says a lot for the LM motive power department at the time that only one Class 7 (later 8) and one Class 6 (later 7) were needed for the duration of the exchanges. Reading through much of the official documentation of the period, it's not entirely clear why the 'Scot' was the only less powerful participant. Why not a 'Lord Nelson' as well, or a 'Castle' (subject to loading gauge restrictions)? It's discussed in the official minute whether the loadings should have been reduced for the Class 6 but in the event it appeared to take whatever its bigger sisters did, in the main with little trouble. Certainly, on the ex-LNER main line, the presence of a powerful 4-6-0 on an express was something new. All the constituents of the LNER (excepting the GER) never used 4-6-0s as principal express motive power, preferring locos with trailing trucks instead. The GNR never built one (it wasn't until the advent of the BR Standard Fives that Doncaster built a 4-6-0), neither did the NBR, and none of the GC express 4-6-0s was as good as a 'Director'. The NER had a decent 4-6-0 mixed traffic loco, but its expresses were handled by Atlantics in the main. The LNER largely carried on with this policy for express work (again the ex-GE was the sole exception) building generations of Pacifics. For the 'secondary' main line work, the wide-firebox V2 was preferred to a big 4-6-0 in the 1930s. Photograph J.C. Flemons, The Transport Treasury.

46162 QUEEN'S WESTMINSTER RIFLEMAN at Scrubs Lane on one of the WR Down test runs, the 1.30pm from Paddington, 25 May 1948. Photograph J.C. Flemons, The Transport Treasury.

THIRTIES FILE

There were few routes more full of interest in the latter half of the 1930s than the Callander & Oban line with its steep gradients, attractive stations and superb scenery. Loads had been increasing steadily and with seven or eight daily summer departures from Oban for Stirling and beyond, as well as a couple of freights and some livestock specials, there was no shortage of opportunities for travel, observation and photographs.

In LMS days, up to 1934, motive power consisted mainly of two Caledonian types; the '55' class of inside cylinder 5ft 0in 4-6-0s built between 1902 and 1906 (LMS Nos.14600-14608) and the '191' class of eight with 5ft 6in coupled wheels, outside cylinders and Walschaerts valve gear. These dated from 1923. By 1935 the '55' class was well past its best with withdrawals under way while the 1923 engines, at no time very capable, had become outclassed even with regular assistance from the redoubtable 2F 0-6-0s, the Jumbos, which were often to the fore.

In August 1934 Stanier Class 5s first arrived on the Highland and, in anticipation, it was decided to transfer the eight HR 'Clans' to the Oban line. Thus in 1934-35 14762 and 14765 had made their homes at Stirling, 14763, 14767, 14768 and 14769 at St Rollox and 14764 and 14766 at Oban. They quickly proved themselves masters of the route,

as always free steaming and strong pullers, although the curves took their toll of the frames. The '191s' were relegated to certain lighter trains, to piloting, to some freight work normally the province of the Jumbos, and the odd working to Ballachulish. In 1935-36 the HR 'Clans' at St Rollox were joined by two Highland 'Castles', 14681 and 14686.

In this delightful photograph by W.A. Camwell, '191' 4-6-0 14622 is assisting 14767 CLAN MACKINNON on an evening train, making an energetic start out of Oban prior to launching themselves at the gruelling 2½ miles at 1 in 50 to Glencruitten Crossing.

Weight restrictions on bridges in the Pass of Leny north of Callander had precluded the use of Stanier Class 5s but in 1939 with strengthening completed the Clans were being displaced. By mid-1940 all had returned to the Highland where plenty of work still awaited them. Withdrawal of the eight Caledonian 4-6-0s started in 1939 but the last survivor, No.14621, soldiered on until 1945. The two Castles remained in the south, latterly at Stirling, until mid-1943.

Nowadays the regular Glasgow to Oban diesel services run over the West Highland line as far as Crianlarich and stations are drastically reduced. But at least scenery is as fine as ever.

From original notes by James Stevenson.

NO(TURNE

A haunter of the dark if ever there was one, George Heiron was almost the only well-known railway photographer of the 1950s to engage in this particular aspect of the art. Added to a remarkable eye for composition, this resulted in some stirring images. Take the lovely Castle at Bristol Temple Meads for instance, 5062 EARL OF SHAFTESBURY with its crew joining in the fun, posed in proper newsreel fashion. At Kings Cross (above) George caught Gateshead A1 60124 KENILWORTH and back at home station Temple Meads again, below, found Bath's 73028 a suitable case for treatment. Catch the ghostly Fireman, caught bending and standing in the tender coal space. Photographs George Heiron, courtesy Mrs Shirley Heiron, The Transport Treasury.

SOU'WEST SURVIVORS
By Keith Miles

With a final fleet of 528 engines operating over a route mileage of 445 plus 131 in joint ownership and a further 27 with running powers, the Glasgow & South Western was not an insignificant partner in the newly formed Northern Division of the LMS in 1923. Nonetheless, so far as locomotive matters were concerned, the centre of power and influence settled upon St Rollox, the senior partner as it were. During the initial settling-in period, therefore, it soon became evident that Caledonian practice with its uniformity of design would prevail and that the disparate, generally small classes of the Sou'West would go to the wall. And so they did; the cull began

immediately and by the early 1930s over 85% of the fleet had disappeared to be replaced, in the main, by the emerging LMS standard classes of Midland origin – see *Truly Great Little Engines*, BYLINES, March 2005.

Until 1912 locomotive development on the G&SWR had progressed in a steady, yet unremarkable fashion and, truth to tell, all but a few of the engines seemed somewhat undersized for the job in hand. The arrival of Peter Drummond from the Highland Railway changed all that. His first design in 1913 was a massive 0-6-0, the biggest and heaviest in Britain at the time and not surpassed in Scotland until the introduction of

Gresley's J38s in 1926. Known as 'Pumpers' by reason of their feed water pumps, they were, not surprisingly, strong engines with an allocated load of fifty wagons on the Long Road Goods, that is between Glasgow and Carlisle via Dalry, as compared with thirty-eight for the earlier Manson engines. Strong they might have been but they were slow, seemingly incapable of keeping time, especially uphill. Furthermore, they had an voracious appetite for coal, and mechanical breakdown of the feed water heating system in the tenders led to a loss of water such that, as David L Smith remarked in his *Tales of the Glasgow & South Western Railway* (Ian Allan, 1961) 'every Pumper was going about like

Whether large or small, the majority of G&SWR locomotives fell to the torch by the mid-1930s. Here at St Enoch in August 1930, one of the biggest, Whitelegg Baltic 15405, reverses out of the station after having brought in an express service from the coast. In the background another of the class dwarfs the appropriately named 'Wee Bogie' 14135, one of Smellie's 119 class built in 1885 for the Greenock services. The 4-4-0 was withdrawn in December 1930 and 15405 in August 1936. Photograph H.C. Casserley.

easier to drive and fire than anyone had ever known'.

The eleven members of the 403 class were built at the NBL's Queens Park Works and in appearance were like a stretched version of the Pumpers with a leading pony truck. 'With the best will in the world I could not bring myself to dub it a handsome locomotive', observed Thomas Middlemass on seeing one for the first time in 1934 (*Mainly Scottish Steam*, David & Charles, 1973). All the principal dimensions were the same, driving wheels, cylinders, boiler, steam pressure and the resultant tractive effort, but the new engines had the advantage of superheating and two combination injectors. For the crews the change in working conditions, according to David L Smith, 'was like a transfer to Heaven after a sojourn in Another Place'. One inconsequential feature was the persistent rumour that the engines had been built for Austria. It seems that NBL had had an Austrian contract but this had been cancelled at the outbreak of World War 1. Some of the accumulated material could feasibly have been used on the 403s but the design was pure Drummond. Nevertheless the engines were dubbed 'Austrian Goods' and the name stuck throughout their working lives. All eleven were allocated to the Sou'West's Carlisle Currock shed and their performance on the Glasgow and Ayrshire coast freight services was said to be truly remarkable. One engine was recorded as running the 128 miles from Glasgow College Goods to Carlisle Midland Yard with fifty wagons south of Johnstone on one tank of water.

Drummond's next design was another winner which to Thomas Middlemass 'appeared substantially enough engineered to have emanated from a marine workshop, much less those of the North British Locomotive Company. Reid's North British 0-6-2 tanks which up to then had formed my Scottish criterion, suddenly seemed terrier-like by comparison'. Much of the work associated with the Ayrshire coalfield was, at that time, in the hands of venerable 0-6-0s which, in the absence of turntables, resulted in considerable tender-first running. Drummond had already designed an 0-6-4T for the Highland Railway and now produced a remarkably similar engine but with the rear bogie

replaced by a pair of radial wheels. The first half-dozen, built in 1915, were sent to Ayr where the long wheelbase initially caused some damage to colliery trackwork, not to mention the occasional derailment – the radial wheels being restricted to a movement of only two inches either side. But there was no denying that they were strong and the dozen delivered in 1917 had a wider distribution; a couple to Ardrossan, three to Corkerhill and seven to Hurlford whence they worked on the direct line between Glasgow and Kilmarnock with its daunting three mile climb at 1 in 67/70 from Barrhead up to milepost 10½.

Drummond, or PD as he was known among the enginemen, ordered a further ten in 1918 but he died in office shortly afterward. Work on the contract had barely commenced so the new Locomotive Superintendent, R H Whitelegg, was able to make some adjustments to the design. He wrote in the October 1951 SLS *Journal* that 'the ten 0-6-2 tank engines of Mr P Drummond's design that were under construction when I came to Kilmarnock appeared to me generally to be quite a good and useful type of engine, and any modifications that I made were of a minor character, the chief being an increase in the water capacity of the tanks, as with a tank engine water capacity is of the greatest importance'. This increase in capacity of only 1800 to 1910 gallons was barely noticeable (unlike his ugly rebuilds of the Manson 14 class 0-6-0Ts) but the feature which picked out the new engines from their predecessors was the typically Whitelegg curved outline of the cab cut-out. On delivery in the summer of 1919 these latest engines went to Hurlford (seven) and Ayr (three).

All eleven 2-6-0s and twenty-eight 0-6-2Ts passed to the LMS becoming Nos.17820-17830 and 16400-16427 all arranged, it would appear, not in order of being built but in age of boiler, a carry over from the Sou'West 1919 renumbering scheme. Almost the first outcome of the grouping, apart from the frenetic winnowing of the locomotive fleet, was the closure of Currock shed in 1924, the complement of fifty or so engines being transferred to the rival establishment at Kingmoor. Here the Austrian Goods found themselves cheek by jowl with their St Rollox equivalents, the five

a watering-cart and you could hardly run from column to column'. Despite copious lubrication (oil consumption was described as 'enormous' in an official letter) heated big end bearings were also a persistent problem and failures became almost a daily occurrence. Needless to say, all this brought about a near revolt among the enginemen which was only averted by the payment of a small bonus to the crews of Pumpers on the Long Road Goods. It must be said, however, that after this turbulent beginning Drummond seemed to see the error of his ways and produced in 1915 what David L Smith described as 'lovely engines, good runners, incredibly economical in coal and water ... the jobs became

LMS numbers	Built	G&SW Orig. 1919	Initial allocations	1933 allocations	Subsequent allocations up to withdrawal (WDN)
16900	5/19	1	Hurlford	Hurlford	12/39 WDN
16901	5/19	2	Hurlford	Hurlford	2/40 Kingmoor Ayr 2/44 WDN
16902	5/19	3	Hurlford	Hurlford	8/35 Blair Athol 12/38 WDN
16903	5/19	4	Hurlford	Stranraer	11/36 WDN Sold to R.McAlpine & Sons
16904	5/19	5	Hurlford	Ardrossan	Sheffield Toton 2/37 WDN Sold to Ashington Coal Co.
16905	6/19	6	Hurlford	Ardrossan	10/37 Workington 1/42 Hurlford 11/45 Kingmoor 4/48 WDN
16906	6/19	7	Hurlford	Ardrossan	Toton 6/38 WDN
16907	6/19	8	Ayr	Ayr	Toton 4/37 Blair Athol 5/39 Beattock 8/39 Kingmoor 11/45 WDN
16908	6/19	9	Ayr	Ayr	6/37 WDN Sold to Ashington Coal Co.
16909	6/19	10	Ayr	Ayr	6/36 WDN
16910	1/16	122 11	Ayr	Ayr	11/36 WDN Sold to R.McAlpine & Sons
16911	6/17	141 12	Hurlford	Hurlford	Workington Barrow 1/37 Upperby 1/42 Hurlford 11/45 Kingmoor 3/46 WDN
16912	6/17	142 13	Hurlford	Ardrossan	Toton 6/38 WDN
16913	6/17	143 14	Hurlford	Hurlford	3/37 Wellingboro' 1/38 WDN
16914	6/17	144 15	Hurlford	Corkerhill	6/37 WDN
16915	6/17	145 16	Hurlford	Hurlford	3/38 WDN
16916	6/17	146 17	Corkerhill	Hurlford	2/36 WDN
16917	6/17	147 18	Corkerhill	Corkerhill	Kingmoor 8/40 WDN
16918	6/17	148 19	Corkerhill	Corkerhill	5/36 WDN
16919	6/17	149 20	Ardrossan	Ardrossan	2/35 Leeds 11/37 WDN
16920	6/17	150 21	Ardrossan	Ardrossan	Toton 9/37 Wellingboro' 1/42 Hurlford 11/45 Kingmoor 11/47 WDN
16921	1/16	284 22	Ayr	Ayr	12/34 Toton 6/35 Stourton Leeds 1/42 Hurlford 11/45 Kingmoor 12/45 WDN
16922	12/15	45 23	Ayr	Ayr	6/35 Stourton 10/35 Toton 5/40 Hasland 1/42 Hurlford 11/45 Kingmoor 12/45 WDN
16923	12/15	84 24	Ayr	Ayr	Kingmoor Toton 1/38 WDN
16924	12/15	90 25	Ayr	Ayr	2/35 Leeds 5/36 WDN
16925	12/15	91 26	Ayr	Ayr	6/35 Stourton 3/36 WDN
16926	5/17	101 27	Hurlford	Ardrossan	2/35 Leeds 1/42 Hurlford 11/45 Kingmoor 12/45 WDN
16927	5/17	102 28	Hurlford	Hurlford	2/38 WDN c43 Stranraer
		└16400-27 1923-25			
17820	11/15	409 51	Currock ✳	Kingmoor	9/35 Corkerhill 1/38 WDN
17821	9/15	403 52	Currock ✳	Kingmoor	9/35 Corkerhill 2/40 Dawsholm 6/43 Corkerhill 9/46 WDN
17822	9/15	404 53	Currock	Kingmoor	9/35 Corkerhill 2/40 Dawsholm Inverness 6/43 Corkerhill 4/44 WDN
17823	10/15	410 54	Currock	Kingmoor	9/35 Ayr 12/36 WDN
17824	9/15	405 55	Currock	Kingmoor	9/35 Ayr 9/35 WDN
17825	9/15	406 56	Currock	Kingmoor	11/36 WDN
17826	9/15	407 57	Currock ✳	Kingmoor	3/36 Carstairs 4/38 Motherwell 2/40 Dawsholm Inverness 3/43 Corkerhill 11/45 WDN
17827	9/15	408 58	Currock ✳	Kingmoor	3/36 Carstairs 4/38 Motherwell 4/38 WDN
17828	11/15	116 59	Currock	Kingmoor	12/35 WDN
17829	11/15	117 60	Currock	Kingmoor	5/38 Motherwell 1/39 WDN 5/42 Inverness 3/43 Corkerhill 3/47 WDN
17830	11/15	121 61	Currock ✳	Corkerhill	11/38 WDN

└ All moved to Kingmoor 6/24   ✳ New CR-type boiler early 1930s   Reinstated   KM 2005

A beautifully sunlit picture of 17821 at its home shed of Kingmoor in the early 1930s. The period can be deduced by the fact that this engine received a new boiler, reputedly of Caledonian pattern, with Ross pop valves in 1931 and the engine beyond it, 14801, was withdrawn in March 1934. This was the erstwhile CR 957, one of Pickersgill's four giant 3-cylinder 4-6-0s of 1921, the largest and most powerful passenger design inherited by the LMS. They did not reach their potential, however, and as early as 1923 14801 had a regular goods turn between Carlisle and Edinburgh and was later frequently seen on the former Sou'West main line. Photograph The Transport Treasury.

Kingmoor in the mid-1930s and 17825 stands in the yard against a backdrop of the towering No.1 pattern coaling plant under construction. The so-called 'Austrian Goods', like the 'Pumpers' before them, incorporated three design innovations. The Sou'West had always been a right-hand drive railway like its Midland partner but Drummond moved the driver to the left-hand side. Also, completely new, he introduced a fusible plug in the firebox and a hosepipe on the footplate. Photograph The Transport Treasury.

2-6-0s of McIntosh's 34 class of 1912, although these were only classified 3F by the LMS whereas the Sou'West engines were 4F. The Caley quintet did similar work to their new companions, express freight services on their southern main line and also to Perth and Dundee. Even in pre-grouping days, however, it had been realised that something bigger was needed and seven of the 1913/14 179 class 4-6-0s were sent to Carlisle and Perth to assist. I was fortunate to see the last two of these (in fact the very last McIntosh 4-6-0s) 17905 and 17908, at St Rollox prior to their being broken up. As for the 0-6-2Ts, they suffered a change in that they were renumbered 16900-16927 in 1925 to make way for the Midland-style standard 0-6-0 shunting tanks being built in large numbers.

Come the watershed of the Motive Power Department reorganisation at the beginning of 1935 there were less than seventy Sou'West engines still running in main line service. Leaving aside the two classes that form the subject of this story, there were but ten of the X2 boiler rebuilds of the 1900 and 1907 Manson 361 class 0-6-0s, five of his later 17 class, nine Drummond superheated 4-4-0s and the five

Whitelegg Baltic tanks. By the end of 1937 all these had disappeared, the Baltics being snuffed out by September 1936 – see *The Sou'West Big Pugs*, BRILL December 2003. During the same period inroads also began to be made into our subject classes and, furthermore, the surviving engines started drifting away from their traditional stamping grounds as indicated in the accompanying table. Of the 2-6-0s one had already moved up to Corkerhill where it took its turn running the 1.00am Glasgow College-Stranraer freight, recording 70mph through Kilkerran on one occasion. It was now followed by another three with two others going to Ayr. The remaining trio ended up at Motherwell where, incidentally, they rejoined the CR 2-6-0s which had arrived in 1935.

The movements among the 0-6-2Ts were altogether more adventurous as they involved transfers not only into other pre-grouping company territories but even into England! I've been unable to discover the actual dates of some of the moves but suffice to say that, commencing in early 1935, no less than fifteen forayed south into Sassenach territory – that Ayrshire patriot, Robert Bruce, Earl of

Carrick, would have been proud of them! A couple went into the nearer Western Division Districts at Workington and Barrow but the remainder penetrated deep into the Midland Division; Leeds, Stourton, Sheffield, Hasland and Toton. It's perhaps worth mentioning in passing that in autumn 1935/spring 1936 nine MR 0-6-4T 'Flatirons' were taken off passenger services and also sent to Toton for shunting and freight duties. 16913 and 16920 travelled even as far south as Wellingborough where George Bushell was a passed cleaner at the time. To him they *seemed large and cumbersome compared to the engines that we were used to but they were strong and with their steam reversing gear they were well suited to the task of shunting loaded coal wagons on the flat. The cab was roomy and comfortable, especially on a winter's night on the top of Henlow embankment.* (*LMS locos from the Footplate*, Bradford Barton). The Henlow Sidings shunt, it would appear, was in the Old Man's Link which, apart from the older drivers after which it was named, had the most senior passed firemen booked into it. It follows, therefore, that the passed cleaners spent a lot of time on their duties when the former were called upon

Left. 17830 had been transferred to Corkerhill from Kingmoor shortly after the whole class had been moved from Currock and was initially involved in running the 1.00am Glasgow College to Stranraer freight, recording 70mph through Kilkerran on occasion. It remained at Corkerhill for the rest of its life; here it is in the yard with the shed's 35 ton shear-legs above the boiler. Beyond is 17266, one of the thirty-five Caley 'Jumbos' built by Neilsons during Dugald Drummond's major reorganisation of St Rollox Works in 1883/4 – see *The Caley*, BRILL Annual No 13. Photograph The Transport Treasury.

Bottom left and below. These photographs illustrate the differences between the original Drummond 0-6-2Ts and the later Whitelegg variants. 16915 was one of three of the class which spent their entire lives based at Hurlford. The remarkable similarity to Drummond's earlier 0-6-4Ts for the Highland Railway is very apparent. Also conspicuous in this view is the novel addition of a footplate hosepipe. The Whitelegg engine, 16900, as it happens another of the lifelong Hurlford trio, has a shorter dome cover, marginally longer and taller side tanks with the filler caps well forward and smaller, rounded-top cab cut-outs. Unseen is the move back to right-hand drive. Photographs E. Scrumpter Collection and The Transport Treasury.

for driving turns. According to George, *Henlow Sidings was the bleakest place on earth in winter, also the heaviest to work as it was flat, all the wagons loaded and all fly shunting.* It was in this regard that a drawback was found to the steam reverser which was, after all, a novelty to Midland men. *No one at top level thought it necessary to issue any instructions regarding its maintenance, therefore nobody knew that there was an hydraulic control cylinder as well as the steam cylinder; consequently, it was never filled with oil. When the reverse control lever was moved over, the main lever would shoot over with a bang and a rattle. I marvelled that nobody got in the way of it and was maimed for life.*

I mentioned earlier that Drummond had produced a class of eight 0-6-4 tanks for the Highland Railway where one of their principal

jobs was banking from Blair Atholl. This was an important staging post for, with very few exceptions, it was the first stopping place for long-distance northbound trains from Perth. Furthermore, the next seventeen miles up to Druimuachdar (1484 ft above sea level) was a fearsome bank having a ruling gradient of 1 in 70. With the dwindling number of the Highland engines, first 16902 was transferred there in 1935 followed by 16907 in 1937. When the work was subsequently taken over by other classes, 16902 was withdrawn but 16907 went south to undertake the same task at Beattock. For whatever reason it didn't remain long, retreating to Kingmoor three months later.

During the war years, not surprisingly perhaps, official transfer notices were not available

but vigilant enthusiasts kept an eye on interesting changes. *The Railway Observer*, therefore, was able to report that all the surviving English-based 0-6-2Ts had returned to Hurlford in January 1942. Similarly, 17829, which had been withdrawn from service in 1939, was reported as being reinstated in May 1942 and sent to Inverness where it joined 17822 and 17826. There they were noted as working on the Elgin line but also, apparently, on the Far North line, being observed at Nigg and Tain. Their reign on the Highland was short-lived, however, and together with the other remaining member of the class, 17821, they were transferred to Corkerhill in the early part of 1943. The *Observer* duly reported the quartet as being 'still at work; one of them, believed to be 17826, being seen at Rutherglen newly painted'. 17822 was withdrawn in April 1944 and less than two years later the six Hurlford 0-6-2Ts, 16905, 16911, 16920, 16921, 16922 and 16926, were shepherded south to join 16907 at Kingmoor.

That is how I found the Sou'West survivors on my arrival in Scotland but it is my great regret that I never actually got to see any of them in action. The tank engines were immured at the far south of the Division and, in any case, were withdrawn almost immediately of which 16907, 16911 and 16926 turned up at the St Rollox Dump in early 1946. The last two went to Kilmarnock in the early summer but, for some reason, 16907 lingered on and was eventually cut up in the Erecting Shop in January 1947. Of the Austrian Goods, 17822 was withdrawn in April 1944 and 17826 in November 1945. This last engine arrived on the Dump in early 1946 where it remained until spring 1947 before going to Kilmarnock. At the same time 17829 arrived at the Works on 8th March 1947 for a full report which led to its withdrawal on the 22nd and the subsequent funereal passage to Kilmarnock in October. Meanwhile, 17821 had been variously described as 'out of use' or 'derelict' at Corkerhill following its withdrawal in September 1946 but it eventually met its fate at Kilmarnock in August 1947.

So, of all the G&SWR engines, only 16905 made the transition into British Railways but it was withdrawn in April 1948 without carrying its new number or identity. Whilst it may have been the last in main line service it was not, in truth, the ultimate Sou'West survivor. Of the two engines sold to Ashington Coal Company in 1937, 16904 wasn't broken up until 1952 and 16908 was still at work in 1955. And, of course, there is still 0-6-0T No.9 (LMS 16379) in the Glasgow Museum of Transport – see *LMS Northern Division Dock Tanks*, BRILL, June and August 2005.

With an unmistakable Midland pattern signal box in the background, 16904 fills up from that same company's style of water crane in Toton Down Sidings in the 1930s. This was one of seven of the class sent to work in or from that huge marshalling yard together with (as it happened) nine disgraced MR 'Flatirons'. 16904 was sold out of service in February 1937 to the Ashington Coal Co. in Northumberland where it wasn't broken up until 1952. Photograph Rex Conway Steam Railway Collection.

First 16902 in August 1935, then 16907 in April 1937, were sent to Blair Atholl for banking duties in place of their Highhland 0-6-4T progenitors. 16902, still in early LMS livery, takes a break beside one of the distinctive stone-based water towers sited at each end of the station. It seems that the 0-6-4Ts had not found favour with the enginemen (too heavy and clumsy, inadequate water capacity and axleboxes always running hot) so the replacements were greeted with some relief.

16923, one of Drummond's first half-dozen and built in December 1915, spent most of its life on home territory at Ayr. In the mid-1930s, however, it went first to Kingmoor, as pictured here, and then to Toton where it was withdrawn in January 1938. It is shown chronologically sandwiched between a Caley Jumbo and a standard LMS engine. Photograph The Transport Treasury.

17824 spent its entire working life at Carlisle, going to Ayr in September 1935 only to be withdrawn almost on arrival. It's parked against one of the original Caley 60s which, by then, had been supplanted from most passenger work by the emerging LMS classes. Photograph The Transport Treasury.

The longest-lived of the Austrian Goods was 17829. After over twenty years at Carlisle it was one of the trio mysteriously moved to Motherwell in 1938 where it was withdrawn less than a year later. After three years (where, I wonder?) it was reinstated in 1942 to help with the war effort and sent to Inverness. It soon returned to the G&SW at Corkerhill where it was withdrawn in March 1947. Another few months were spent rusting away at St Rollox before going to Kilmarnock for breaking up in October. Photograph The Transport Treasury.

In Threes

Mid-morning at Laira shed in early 1954; three Kings line up awaiting their next turns of duty. The nearest is 6004 KING GEORGE III, a recent transfer from Wolverhampton Stafford Road in exchange for Laira's 6014. It had recently worked the up 8.30am Plymouth-London and still bears the chalked '605' Reporting Number on the smokebox door. In the middle is 6012 KING EDWARD VI and, furthest away, 6023 KING EDWARD II carrying a 'Cornish Riviera' headboard for the up working at 12.30pm from North Road. Photograph Peter Kerslake.

Three Castles now, at Laira again and all visitors, at teatime on Sunday 20 May 1956. Nearest is Canton's 5054 EARL OF DUCIE, centre is Bath Road's 5063 EARL BALDWIN while the third, 4099 KILGERRAN CASTLE, hails from Penzance. Devonport dockyard was open to the public that Whitsuntide ('Navy Days' were major annual events then) and a number of reliefs had brought visitors from far and wide. The engines returned with their charges later in the day. Photograph Peter Kerslake.

Axminster Days
Notes by E.S. Youldon

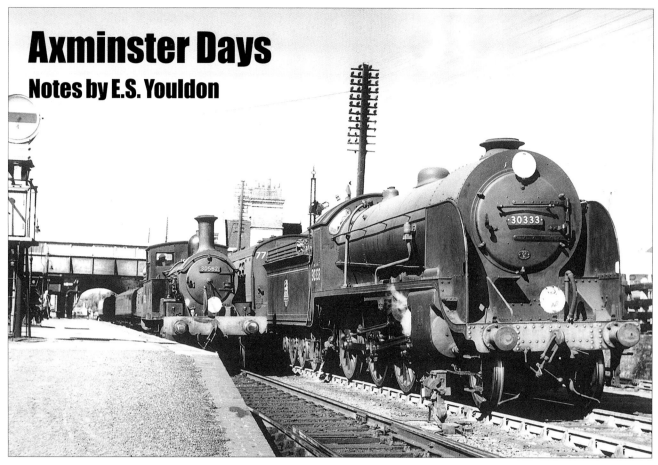

H15 4-6-0 30333 departs on 26 July 1956 with the 3.36pm Templecombe to Exeter Central stopper having dropped rear 'TC' (Through Carriages) for Lyme Regis. These latter vehicles had departed Waterloo on the 1.0pm express and transferred to the 3.36 at Templecombe. Adams tank 30582 will run forward, back on to the detached coaches and after four reversals with them in tow, depart for the seaside. Photograph David Anderson.

A more normal scene in July 1956, with Adams 0415 class 4-4-2T backing on to the Lyme Regis branch set for its next sortie to the coast. Photograph David Anderson.

Merchant Navy Pacific 35010 BLUE STAR pulls away with an up Waterloo train. Photograph David Anderson.

Rebuilt West Country 34048 CREDITON approaches with what is probably the 6.5pm Exeter Central to Clapham Junction Milk in May 1963. An unsecured cab gangway door on CREDITON has swung outwards! The Lyme branch curves sharply off to the right to cross the main line on the flyover in the background. Photograph David Anderson.

Salisbury's Standard Class 4 2-6-0 76017 arrives with a down local goods in May 1963. On this job there was no guarantee that the engine would actually reach Exmouth Junction, so the practice was to run down tender first. Photograph David Anderson.

West Country 34091 WEYMOUTH has a cushy time with an up local goods in May 1963. The ground frame in the foreground was for switching the branch loco when running round its train. Photograph David Anderson.

Battle of Britain 34061 73 SQUADRON departs with a down stopping service in May 1963. The casing definitely looks to have suffered some form of slow motion yard collision. Photograph David Anderson.

Battle of Britain 34051 WINSTON CHURCHILL restarts what looks like the 3.5pm Salisbury to Exeter Central stopper. Fire buckets, barley sugar gas lamps, tip-up barrow and LSWR box 'complete a timeless scene' as the familiar expression has it. Photograph David Anderson.

An Exmouth Junction Standard 2-6-4T, 80041, departs with freight form the reversing siding and, with the signal cleared for the up main, will proceed briskly towards Chard Junction. Photograph David Anderson.

Trans Pennine Summer Evening

Bryan Wilson

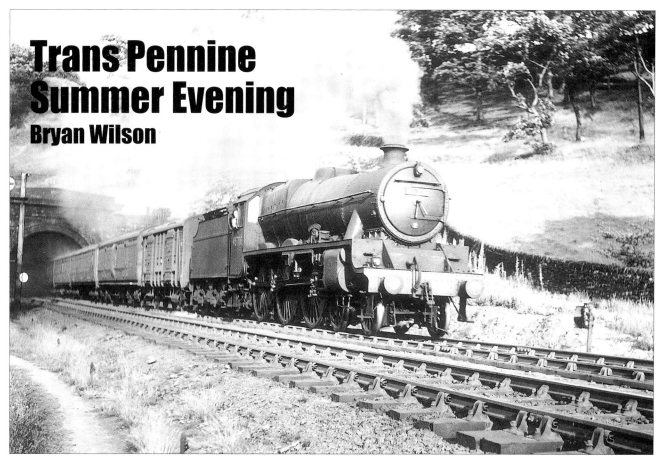

The evening sun glints (well almost) on the west portal of the 657 yard Sowerby Bridge tunnel on the Calder Valley main line, some time about 1949. First to emerge is Newton Heath Jubilee 45706 EXPRESS with a train of mixed and grubby empty news vans for Manchester (Red Bank) sidings. EXPRESS spent over twenty years at 26A and carried her Fowler tender until September 1958. The banner signal by the tunnel mouth is the repeater for Sowerby Bridge West down home signal. At its foot is a 'C' board marking the commencement of a temporary speed restriction – such boards have long since been superseded by the present signs showing the actual speed permitted. The following train (lower) is the evening Bradford and Leeds to Southport service which joined portions at Low Moor. This was the return working of the 1.0pm Southport-Bradford. The loco is almost new Black 5 44737 of Southport; the stock is pure LMS.

A Touch of Optimism: Dringhouses Yard

Above. The 'birds eye view' of the Yard from the top of a lighting pole near the hump. We are looking south with the Control Tower on the immediate left with the additional east side sidings in the murk behind and left of it. The four running lines to the right of the yard are (left-right) Up and Down Main and Up and Down Leeds. The Down sidings are in the murk beyond.

Dringhouses marshalling yard, located on the Up side of the East Coast Main Line south of York station, was constructed in 1915/16 to deal with increasing traffic in the First World War. It had 20 through roads. In 1961 it was converted to a 'hump' yard; some sidings were lengthened and nine additional ones provided on the east side – such was the optimistic outlook for wagon load goods traffic at that time.

An elevated modern control room was constructed at the north end of the hump yard from which the operator set routes into the appropriate sidings for the wagons, controlling their speed by means of the hydraulically activated retarders. Dringhouses was the first marshalling yard in the country to deal exclusively with fully braked express goods trains. It should be noted that there was a small 'Dringhouses Down Yard' which consisted of just four through reception roads on the Down side of the main lines. Our photographs were taken in 'deep mid-winter' conditions although it was still officially autumn on 15th December 1961, soon after modernisation.

Notes by Bryan Wilson.

Above. Still looking south but now in close-up. The retarders 'nip' the wagon wheels at varying pressures as they roll off the hump and are controlled into the sidings to avoid heavy impact or, worse still, running out foul of other vehicles at the far end. As befits a modern yard, the place is clean and tidy. Note the absence of things to fall over, mainly due to the hydraulic operation of the points.

Left. Retarders in close-up. This view is looking north towards the hump with its stabled diesel shunter. Not much happening but then, much of the fitted freight work was in the evening and night hours. This method of working lasted until 3rd March 1985 on which date hump shunting ceased and the Control Tower closed. The yard itself lasted for another two years after which its work was transferred to Doncaster. A housing estate now occupies much of the site.

Fourum Down Weston Way

Weston-Super-Mare had a pleasant little station on a curve, together with further platforms for excursions and associated sidings for stock and engine purposes. The line had originally been a branch and the first purpose of the excursion platform had been to separate the Bristol riff-raff on their cheap tickets from the rest of the clientele. These two pictures show the main station, 'General' with (top) 7018 DRYSLLWYN CASTLE arriving from Bristol on a summer Sunday in 1959 and (below) 6999 CAPEL DEWI HALL running through with stock on Saturday 17 February 1962. Photographs Peter Barnfield.

To the north and west of General station was 'Locking Road' station; it comprised the two main platforms visible here, designed to process the excursionist hordes in and out of the town. For this business, Weston was effectively worked as a branch, as it had in broad gauge days. Somewhere behind the steam and smoke in the distance is the little engine shed; there was an 0-6-0PT (in 1947 at least) and a Saint and a Castle. This was surely the most peculiar allocation for a one road shed, or a shed anywhere really. The turntable and water tanks were of a scale to service the numerous visiting locos on a summer Saturday but there was no coal stage. On Saturday 21 July 1962 (top) Ivatt 2-6-2T 41245 was station pilot; nearest of the excursion engines was 5041 TIVERTON HALL. Below, in 1959 two Halls were on the service lines, 4941 LLANGEDWYN HALL (left) and 4954 PLAISH HALL. Photographs Peter Barnfield.

Riley's Railway Roundabout

North Wales and the Borderlands 21st July 1951
Notes by Bryan Wilson

Our journey begins at Gobowen where 'Auto' pannier 6404 of Croes Newydd calls with the 10.35am Oswestry-Wrexham local. The trailer is W227, almost brand new in 'carmine and cream'. It stayed in the area for eight years. Note the small destination board above the second door and the distinctive windows with sliding ventilators. Passengers for up trains climb the stairs beneath two delightful 'finger' signs. Photograph R.C. Riley, The Transport Treasury.

Next to arrive is a scruffy 7008 SWANSEA CASTLE with the 9.30am Birkenhead to Bournemouth complete with SR stock. This is Oxford shed's contribution to the working which it shared with Chester on an alternate day basis. The Train Reporting Number, 928, follows the rule that any train starting or finishing its journey away from the WR should be prefixed by a '9'. Gobowen, unusually, has two (different) running-in boards on the up side. Photograph R.C. Riley, The Transport Treasury.

The branch line side of Gobowen with 0-4-2T 1459 of Oswestry in 'sandwich' formation for the next trip home. The leading car is brand new W231 followed by composite driving trailer W6820 of October 1936. On the other side of the loco is W210, rebuilt from a steam rail motor 91 in 1935. What is more, each coach is in a different livery; W231, a BR car, in red and cream, W6820 in red and W210 brown and cream. The nameboard ALL CHANGE was well photographed, and possibly unique. Photograph R.C. Riley, The Transport Treasury.

Pannier tank 2188 of the small 2181 class sits just north of Wrexham General station. The 2181s, rebuilt from 2021s, had increased brake power for work at Stourbridge, Croes Newydd and St Blazey, which all involved steep gradients. Croes Newydd usually had three, at this time 2185, 2186 and 2188. No smokebox door numberplate yet and GWR number on the buffer beam. She lasted until February 1952. Photograph R.C. Riley, The Transport Treasury.

A 'close up' look at the penultimate 6878 LONGFORD GRANGE, one of Birkenhead's regulars for the 'night Bordesley'. These locos were strong, free running and popular and could turn their hand to anything. This time it's the 11.00am return trip from Hafod Siding (Johnstown) which has just arrived in Croes Newydd Yard. Photograph R.C. Riley, The Transport Treasury.

'Dukedog' 9013 of Machynlleth ready to depart from Ellesmere (Salop) with the 12.30pm Welshpool to Whitchurch which, like many trains on the route, spent half an hour at Oswestry. A fine parachute water column overlooks the scene. Photograph R.C. Riley, The Transport Treasury.

Another 'Dukedog', 9024 of Machynlleth, runs into Ellesmere with the 2.05pm Whitchurch-Welshpool. This also has the number on the buffer beam and, you'd suspect, 'GWR' on the tender. Note the token set down and pick up points by the first coach. The train adjacent, waiting access to the single line, is the 11.00am Aberystwyth-Manchester (London Road) – with a portion from Barmouth – headed by 7820 DINMORE MANOR; that coach M12933, a third corridor, is only two years old. The 2.40pm 'Auto' to Wrexham waits in the spur beyond, by the overbridge. Photograph R.C. Riley, The Transport Treasury.

Non-auto 0-4-2T 5812, again still in GWR style, runs in with the afternoon train from Gobowen which was 'worked by Llanfyllin branch engine and coaches' according to the Working Timetable. The engine was but the coaches weren't as we will see later. The long bridge was the official entrance to the Works from Gobowen Road. Photograph R.C. Riley, The Transport Treasury.

Local 'Dukedog' 9001 broadside in the shed with a local engineman's two wheeled transport by the front bogie. Look how well kept the shed is – spotless. The 4-4-0 still carries a 'Duke' chimney, which makes it look even more ancient. Photograph R.C. Riley, The Transport Treasury.

Part of the shed's responsibilities was to provide for breakdowns. This is clerestory coach MPD 94, which looks like the riding van, tucked away in the sidings. Photograph R.C. Riley, The Transport Treasury.

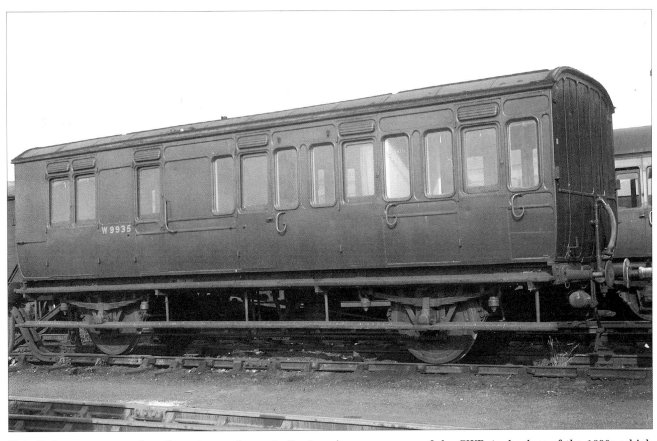

This little gem, captured at Oswestry, and now in Engineer's use, was one of the GWR 4 wheelers of the 1890s which was converted to a Camping Coach in 1938 just two years before such attractions were withdrawn for the duration of the War. As it turned out, the vehicle survived longer in Departmental use than it did as a Camping Coach. In any event, the 'Camping' number W9935 was retained. Photograph R.C. Riley, The Transport Treasury.

As mentioned above, 5812 'swopped' its coaches at Oswestry for one of the proper Llanfyllin branch 2-car close coupled 'B' sets. Nos.W6776, W6777 and W6887, W6888, were the regular vehicles, being suitably marked on the coach ends – as can just be seen here behind the loco cab roof. The cattle pens are behind the train (right) and beyond is the engine shed, which closed 27 September 1952; after that date the branch loco ran right through to and from Oswestry – another doubtful economy. Photograph R.C. Riley, The Transport Treasury.

Llanfyllin Goods Yard with a row of 'Iron Minks' for Internal Use Only; effectively, sheds on wheels. There are two varieties on show; five have their original doors and three have replacement wooden ones. In the distance 5812 takes a drink down by the shed in the eleven minutes allowed. Photograph R.C. Riley, The Transport Treasury.

Back at Oswestry and local Cambrian 0-6-0 887 – with only four months left – has re-engined the 4.10pm Whitchurch-Welshpool during the (statutory) half hour here. Photograph R.C. Riley, The Transport Treasury.

Table 184 of the Western Region Public Timetable declared that 'Additional trains are run between Oswestry and Tinkers Green Halt – see local announcements'. These were for those 'Gunners' incarcerated at Park Hall Camp, so they could partake of the pleasures available in Town. Here is one such train, the 5.40pm departure from Oswestry with 1428 and Trailer W118 next to it, still in GW livery. This was another conversion from a steam rail motor – it spent its last years as a classroom at Monmouth. The train would do the trip to Tinker's Green and be back here in 8½ minutes. Photograph R.C. Riley, The Transport Treasury.

Our day is nearly over and locos are gathering on Chester (GW) shed for the night. First in view is 6828 TRELLECH GRANGE from Stourbridge, rather work-stained shall we say. Behind it is Chester's own 5027 FARLEIGH CASTLE in better shape. The 'char' has been cleared from the smokebox but not yet swept off the buffer beam. Photograph R.C. Riley, The Transport Treasury.

Chester was a regular home for the 'Saint' class, with no less than seven allocated as far back as 1932, once the 'Castles' had taken over the heavier main line work. Here is 2926 SAINT NICHOLAS with just two months left; nevertheless, someone has polished the beading round the splashers. And what a nice LNWR ground signal by the tender end – operated by Chester No.4 Box. Photograph R.C. Riley, The Transport Treasury.

And finally, Dean Goods 0-6-0 2513, another local resident. She stayed until November 1954 then spent her last eight months on the Mid Wales at Brecon. Photograph R.C. Riley, The Transport Treasury.

A4s at York, 18th July 1960

There was an eerie quality to York, as the episodic exhaust beats of slow moving engines rose up to that great roof, rather after the fashion of Kings Cross. With trains in one of the main platforms the unwary, caught too far from the footbridge, might even miss an engine working through. There was always something going on though of course there were 'suspended' moments of quiet and stillness, just as at any other great station. The curving through roads were part of the glory and all manner of activity took place on them. Top, 60029 WOODCOCK runs through with The Flying Scotsman bound for the north. Below, 60014 SILVER LINK (34A Kings Cross) is ready to come off a down Tyne Commission Quay train while 60019 BITTERN (52A Gateshead) waits to take over. Photographs J.D. Leahy.

The Western Side of Shrewsbury
Notes by Bryan Wilson

7013 BRISTOL CASTLE (the old 4082 in disguise) backs onto the up Cambrian Coast Express. It has a double chimney and smokebox reservoir for the mechanical lubricator – which does not improve its looks – but carries the attractive 1956-style headboard. Photograph Paul Chancellor Collection.

On the Western, when it came to double heading at busy times, any combination would do. This time it's 6856 STOWE GRANGE of Worcester leading Britannia Pacific 70016 ARIEL of Canton. They are heading away from Shrewsbury with a North to West express of mixed GW and LM stock, as appropriate for a Joint line. Photograph Paul Chancellor Collection.

The massive Severn Bridge Junction Box towers above Collett 0-6-0 2209 with a Class 'H' goods which includes a breakdown crane. This is 'in transit' as distinct from on its way to or from a mishap – this would be indicated by an 'A' or 'B' headcode. Little 2209 was something of a wanderer and included Neyland and Ebbw Junction on its 'CV', apart from four different sheds in the 84 Division. Note the large SHREWSBURY board on the box and the minute SEVERN BRIDGE JUNCTION high above it, beneath the fire escape. Photograph Paul Chancellor Collection.

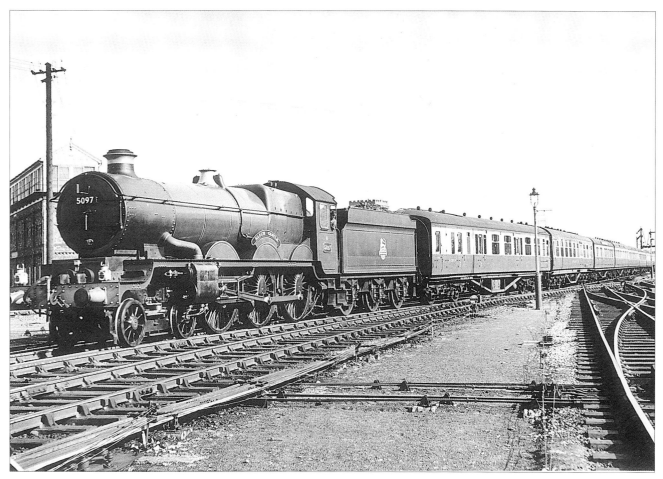

For those 'spotting' in London, 5097 SARUM CASTLE was one of the hardest Castles to find. It spent twenty years at Shrewsbury and most of its post-war time on the 'Double Home' turn to Newton Abbot with the Liverpool-Plymouth services, which it shared with Castles from Newton Abbot. Here she is arriving on the northbound service with a pleasing signal gantry in the background. Photograph Paul Chancellor Collection.

7019 FOWEY CASTLE, a Bath Road engine for the first twelve years of its life, receiving some attention alongside the Western Region coaling stage. Separate coaling for WR and LM sides was the order of the day into the 1960s. The building behind is a legacy of Joint GWR/LNWR arrangements, in the shape of the ancient Shrewsbury & Hereford Railway offices. Photograph Paul Chancellor Collection.

On the other side of the coal stage, local County 4-6-0 1003 COUNTY OF WILTS awaits its next journey north. She is outside the 1855 Shrewsbury & Hereford Railway shed which was shared between the LNW and GW. When the new LNW shed alongside opened in the 1870s, the GWR took over all five roads here. Photograph Paul Chancellor Collection.

A broadside of Chester's 6901 ARLEY HALL with her scarred Hawksworth tender – another of those slow motion yard 'encounters'. It was a long-standing 84 Division engine until the 'purge' to replace GW engines at Chester by Standard Class 5s in August 1958; after that it moved to Canton. Photograph Paul Chancellor Collection.

How Pretty is That?

The late Paul Hocquard took many wonderful pictures and though his negatives were saved, unfortunately any detail as to location, dates and the rest has been lost. The detective work here should not be too difficult, however. The withdrawal of 30199 from Exmouth Junction along with 30225 at the end of 1962 rendered the mainland O2 0-4-4Ts extinct while the Z 0-8-0T next in line (a vast contrast indeed) was taken out of service only a few weeks earlier. It had been at Exmouth Junction with the other Zs for banking since 1959. Clearly this is Exmouth Junction shed and while 30199 might well be on the point of withdrawal it looks in perfect nick otherwise – there's even a water drip visible on the original print. Yet 30952 *has* had its shedplate removed... So do we settle for late 1962, between the big engine's withdrawal and the withdrawal of the little one? Photographs Paul Hocquard, The Transport Treasury.

SIGNALLING PROGRESS ON THE NORTH WEST FRONT
BRYAN WILSON

Starting at the south end of Wigan North Western in 1940, the photographer is standing in the Up Fast – with lookout we hope –looking towards Springs Branch. The two lines on the left are the Up and Down East Goods and those to the right the Up and Down Slow. The signal is 'clear' for the Up Slow. The box behind the Up Fast signals is the old Wigan No.1, a product of the 1894 widening scheme from Springs Branch to Wigan. *Some of these pictures are excessively gloomy – rather more than we'd like – but this type of wartime view is very, very scarce. We hope the interest overcomes the relative lack of quality.*

In the wake of the 'Depression' years of the 1930s, the Government of the day made money available for works which 'were of public benefit'. Amongst these were resignalling schemes for Euston-Willesden, Birmingham, Crewe, Preston, Rugby, Stafford, Warrington and Wigan. Resources available naturally dictated the speed at which such projects could be implemented and at the outbreak of war in 1939, only the work at Rugby had been completed. The work at Crewe and Wigan and in the London suburbs was nearly done and at these places, the work was pursued through to completion.

The Wigan scheme involved the construction of three 'Air Raid Precaution' boxes. These were Wigan No.1 at the south end of Wigan North Western station, No.2 at the north end and Wallgate, west of the former L&Y Wallgate station. The specification was for 14 inch solid brick walls, 12 inch thick reinforced concrete roof with no locking room windows. Even the nameboards were concrete panels. Once the boxes were complete, the new works came into operation between July 1941 and May 1942.

On 26th and 27th July 1941 the 'L&Y' side was dealt with. In this stage, the new Wallgate box opened while Wigan L&Y Nos.2, 3, 4 and 5 were dispensed with. The boxes displaced contained in total 129 levers.

On 31st August 1941 the 'concrete wonder' at the north end of Wigan North Western station opened. At this stage, it only replaced the existing Wigan LNW No.4 and Turners Siding to the north. It was titled No.4 for the time being.

Lastly, on 24th May 1942, Wigan Nos.1 and 2 (LNW boxes) on the main line closed together with L&Y No.1 and Ince Hall on the Central. The new Wigan No.1 opened. Also, on this date, to get the numbering in sequence, the new No.4 at the north end became No.2.

The new No.1 contained two frames of 85 and 40 levers dealing with the main line and L&Y side respectively, plus a total of 105 signal switches, while No.2 contained 65 levers and 14 switches. Down at Wallgate, the new box had a 75 lever conventional frame.

To complete the story, Wigan 1 and 2 concrete boxes closed on 1st October 1972 with the area passing to Warrington Power Box. However, Wigan Wallgate is still with us, having had a replacement frame in 1977 (most of it second-hand, displaced from Bamfurlong Junction in 1972) and a 'panel' from October 2004.

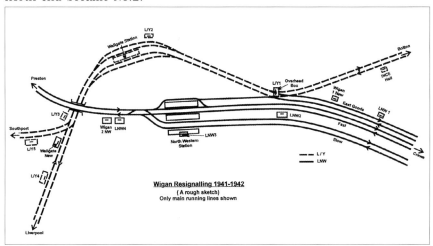

Wigan Resignalling 1941-1942
(A rough sketch)
Only main running lines shown

The view from the south end of Platform One at Wigan North Western before resignalling. The L&Y goods shed is extreme left and a 'Lanky A' 0-6-0 sits at the coal yard outlet with a featherweight load and a vintage Midland Railway brake van. The painted panel high on the van's side for the number can be seen, as can the remains of the tablet racks which once carried the train control codes in the form of inserted tablets (just left of the front entrance). The L&Y's No.1 Box is behind the parachute water column – note that the LNW did things differently, with platform mounted columns – while the LNW's No.2 Box takes (distant) centre stage. The elevated structure to the right is not a box but the luggage hoist at the end of platform 2. As for the signals, they are pure LNW artistry, the majority of them 'fixed' distants. Only that from platform 1 to the Up Fast seems to be operable. We know it is 1941 but camouflaging seems to have been taken a bit far as the nameboard on the gas lamp this side of the hoist is 'Hovis'. That should confuse the enemy!

Over to the west side of the station. LNW No.2 Box centre and the LNW goods shed to the right. Some more attractive signals including the 'shunt ahead' small arms. one of which is 'off', presumably at the behest of the Signal & Telegraph Dept. who are well represented both above and below the gantry.

The sheer size of No.2 Box can be appreciated in this view from the Down side. 148 levers, of which 130 were working when it came into use. The pilot is pushing some vans into No.4 Bay but those on the ground are not unduly perturbed, presumably 'It always misses us'. To the left, former 'Butterley' and 'Yorkshire Main' wagons serve the Gas Works.

The LNW 'tumbler' frame of 148 levers in No.2 Box looks to be in sets of 18 and 16 to allow for the girders laid underneath. There were fixings attached to the girders and where they met a space in the frame above necessarily arose. Hence the gaps seen in the frame, usually of 11 inches. In this case it is beyond lever 34. The movable flap above lever 13 (it's that curious disk) is operated by No.1 box when his Up Fast Distant is cleared. Local instructions would not allow No.2 to clear its Up Fast Distant until this indication was received – all due to braking distances where boxes were close together.

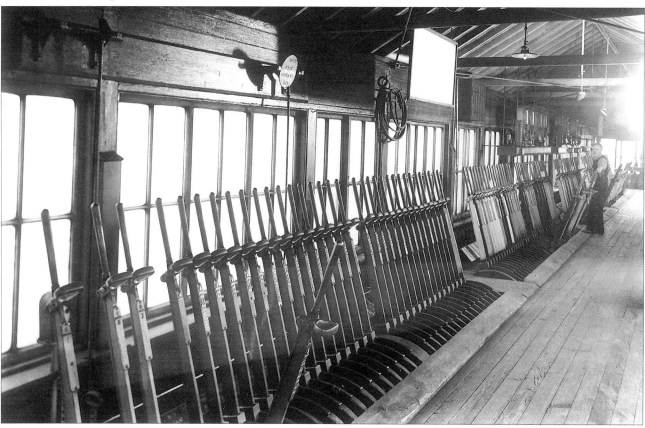

We have progressed to the north end of Wigan North Western station and indeed are looking towards the station from the bridge which carries the LNW main line over the L&Y 'opposition' at the west end of their Wallgate station. The new concrete Wigan No.2 Box is in situ with the old LNW No.4 of 1894 behind it. The new box was titled No.4 between August 1941 and May 1942 until the scheme was completed. The signals ahead, applying to the Up Main read (left to right): to Up Loop (platform 1), Up Main, to Bay 5 and to Up Slow platform 4.

Back at North Western station and looking north in 1941, through the unfortunate blemish of a cracked glass plate. This is the overbridge which crosses the main thoroughfare 'Wallgate'. The notice attached to the water column refers to 'discharge of water onto the public highway'. There appears to be no similar sign on the Down Slow column. The signals are a mix of LNW (left) and LMS.

Looking north from the Down Fast platform it is still very much a 'pre-grouping' scene with LNW signals, an LNW box ahead (No.4, with its replacement beyond) and an LNW van in the Up train arriving into No.1 platform. The water column claims to be No.647. Now who had a list of these we wonder, and can anyone claim to have spotted them all?

Turning to L&Y affairs, this is the view from the LNW's No.2 Box showing the whole of the south end of the North Western station; to the right is the L&Y Wigan No.1 'overhead' box, again of 1894 vintage. Beneath and beyond the box are the lines dropping down to Wallgate station to the right of the coal yard which is situated between the two railways.

'Down below' at the L&Y's Wallgate station looking through the bridge beneath Wallgate itself while L&Y 2-4-2T 10827 sits in the Up platform with passenger stock. This loco did not see the war out. being condemned in January 1944. The box at the other end of the bridge is the old Wigan L&Y No.2.

The interior of Wigan Wallgate box in September 1942. It was situated in the fork of the Liverpool and Southport lines west of Wallgate station and had been open for about 14 months when this view was taken. It is a 75 lever frame although not all levers were fitted. The frame was replaced in 1977 by one from Bamfurlong Junction, displace there in 1972. This in turn lasted until October 2004 when a modern 'NX' panel was installed.

DIESEL DAWN Eastern Region Arrivals
Notes by Peter Kemmett

'The Unexpected' was always to be expected with BR's new diesels and the Eastern Region was no exception. Its twenty Sulzer Type 2s (D5300-D5319) were banned from the Widened Lines because they were more than four tons over the estimated weight! Which was a shame, for they were reported as good performers with no serious problems. That in itself was something of an achievement but when in mid-1959 the further production run of these machines, D5320-D5346, began going to Scotland it was decided to send the Eastern Region ones there too. Top, D5307 comes south through Hatfield with a train from Cambridge on 23 May 1959, past a WD which looks to be 90598 while (below) a very new example stands at Kings Cross next to one of its forebears, N2 0-6-2T 69583. Photographs Frank Hornby and Peter Barnfield.

In 1959 the ER was supposed to have forty Type 2s for the new dieselised suburban working. Typically it only got thirty for the beginning of the summer timetable, so that Hitchin shed continued with steam. Just as typically, it was lumbered with two completely different types from different builders, the Sulzers and the NBL D6100s which could hardly have shared a single spare part between them. The odd bolt, maybe. There were ten 'Baby Deltics' arriving but these represented yet a third completely different type and they too had proved too heavy for the Widened Lines! There were also disturbing signs of troubles to come with these too... Top is D6105 at Kings Cross and below is D6103 at Cambridge with the 5.15pm to Kings Cross. The Eastern got its own back for the loss of the Sulzers by palming the D6100s off on the Scottish Region from 1960. Photographs Terry R. Smith (The Transport Treasury) and Frank Hornby.

D6105 again, light at Hatfield on 23 May 1959. The locos never even 'looked' right; *spoked* wheels? On 13 March 1959 D6105 had 'been booked to work eight bogies Doncaster and back' as a trial but, ominously 'did not run'. In the lower view D6103 has empty stock bound for Kings Cross at Hornsey on 6 June 1959. Ally Pally, as usual, dominates the skyline. See IRWELL PRESS there at the Festival of Railway Modelling, 1-2 April 2006. Photographs Frank Hornby.

What finally saved the ER's suburban bacon was the Brush Type 2 (though as a design its road was as rocky as any) and the BR Sulzer D5000s. Operating the GN suburban service would see a good many more tears yet. The great part of the first Brush locos, however, the D5500s, went to the GE Section where, bizarrely, two were delivered in experimental liveries. D5579 (shown here at Stratford, on 27 February 1960) was in 'golden ochre' ('orange' in local parlance; it is hilarious to imagine a Stratford fitter exclaiming 'I say, is that golden ochre I see before me?') while D5578 had light blue. Were those headcodes deliberate? OMO was another popular one... Given that BR had settled on the main 'pilot' types years before (the first Brush Type 2s had been ordered *in 1955* along with others) it was odd that 'prototypes' were still emerging in 1961. Below is D0280 FALCON at Kings Cross on 7 July 1962, retiring to the 'loco' just as generations of Atlantics and Pacifics had done for decades. The pork barrel politics that saw BR's diesel orders expended on every firm and its dog in every corner of the country in order to secure the British locomotive building industry and the votes of those who worked in it, in the end, destroyed it. Photographs the late W.G. Boyden (courtesy Frank Hornby and Frank Hornby.

Glimpses

A true glimpse. One of the G&SW Section 2P 4-4-0s, in beautiful condition, 'near Kilmarnock' on 29 June 1957. The engine has a Hurlford (67B) plate but even the general distinction which characterised the 4-4-0s of the former G&SW sheds hardly explains this level of exactitude; even the lamp has the engine's number stencilled on it. A Royal pilot? Photograph R. Wilson, The Transport Treasury.

Scotland again and BR Standard 2-6-4T 80004, a Kittybrewster engine since new, conceals itself at Aberdeen station on 29 July 1953. Photograph R. Wilson, The Transport Treasury.

A 4F, 44210, 'somewhere in England'. The intimate little portrait is by Paul Hocquard, so we no not where exactly. A free year's subscription to *British Railways Illustrated* for the first reader to put us out of our misery. Photograph Paul Hocquard, The Transport Treasury.

The East Birmingham Tangle

Notes by Bryan Wilson **All photographs by J.C. Flemons, taken 17th/18th August 1949; courtesy The Transport Treasury**

The London & Birmingham Railway opened its line from Birmingham to Rugby for goods traffic on 12th November 1837 with passengers following on 9th April 1838. Through running to Euston came on 17th September that year. The 'Grand Junction' Railway, in conjunction with the 'Liverpool & Manchester' had reached Vauxhall on the outskirts of Birmingham in July 1837 and was extended to the L&B station in November 1838. Meanwhile the Birmingham & Derby Junction Railway (one of the constituents of the Midland)

reached Lawley Street, east of Curzon Street, by its own line from Whitacre on 10th February 1842. Since 1838, Birmingham & Derby Junction services had run to Birmingham by reversing at Hampton in Arden.

Meanwhile, once Landor Street viaduct and curve were constructed in 1851, the Midland had access to Curzon Street by connection with the L&NWR at what became 'Derby Junction' and the Midland then closed Lawley Street as a passenger station, on 1st May 1851. It used Curzon Street until 1854, when all

normal traffic moved to New Street with Curzon Street thereafter remaining open only for goods and some excursion traffic. It should be noted that Curzon Street was in the timetables as plain 'Birmingham' until Snow Hill station was opened in 1852.

Birmingham's main station, New Street, opened for LNW services to the east on 1st June 1854, local services to Wolverhampton having run from a temporary wooden platform at the west end since 1st July 1852. Its opening resulted in the closure of Curzon Street to

We are looking towards New Street through the signal gantry containing the Up Inner Home signals and Down Starters at Proof House Junction. The 'new' (1896) viaduct lines are on the right and the Midland on the left. Don't by misled by 'Mitchell & Butlers No.3 Bonded Stores'. The actual stores are out of view to the right at a lower level. The signs were on the roof of the 'fish landing' where they could be seen by passing passengers. The fish landing was originally the Excursion station, used until the 1890s. Note the lamp man performing acrobatics on the second signal arm from the left.

was also to be quadrupled from Aston inwards. The shortage of available space led to a new viaduct being built on the top of the original one between Vauxhall and Proof House Junction, where the Aston (Grand Junction) line met the main line from London. The new viaduct allowed Curzon Street traffic to arrive, depart and shunt without crossing the Aston passenger lines on the level. This came into use on 7th May 1893 and as a 'double deck' viaduct, is possibly unique. Further east, the connection with the Midland line to and from Derby and Gloucester were all on the level with the consequent delays and inflexibility. Between 1893 and 1896 therefore, a new curve from Landor Street Junction south of Saltley replaced the 1851 viaduct connection with the LNWR and passed under the LNW main lines and the Up Gloucester line to emerge south of them at what became Grand Junction, where a new signal box opened on 26th April 1896. At the same time, the Gloucester line curves were slewed and altered to locate one each side of the new Derby spur.

Nearer New Street, a new double line viaduct was built on the north side of the 'Proof House' – where guns were tested and certified, hence the name. Further west, by Fazeley Street, the existing formation was widened on the south side, due to the room available, resulting in the dog leg curve we have today on the New Street approach lines. The resulting layout gave separate Up and Down Midland lines into their new side of New Street station, with the LNW keeping to the north side lines. All this work was completed by 1896.

Finally, mention must be made of the 'Line that never was', and if it had been used it would have made the 'Tangle' even more complicated. Following the amalgamation of the Grand Junction and the Liverpool & Manchester in 1845, Huish, the Secretary of the Grand Junction, wanted the London & Birmingham to join his enterprise. Meanwhile, the GW had opened its line from Didcot to Oxford, on 10th June 1844 with intentions to fill the gap that existed further north. The L&B responded by proposing a Tring, Worcester, Dudley and Wolverhampton line.

Huish supported the GW lines in an effort to get the London & Birmingham to co-operate but, not being successful, he proposed a 'Birmingham & Oxford Junction Railway, which would leave an Oxford and Rugby line north of Fenny Compton and run to Curzon Street. Parliament of the day was happy with this proposal; after all, it created some early competition, but it threw the London & Birmingham's Wolverhampton ambitions out. This made the L&B keen to get into the Huish Joint fold – which it did, to form the London & North Western Railway, but it left the 'unfinished business' of the Birmingham & Oxford Junction Railway which, having been passed, had to be built.

The Birmingham & Oxford Junction Railway Act provided for the railway to run to Great Charles Street (Snow Hill) with a branch to Curzon Street. Huish, being the character he was, got the Act altered to make the Curzon Street 'branch' the main line and the Snow Hill line the subject of a separate Act. The Main Line (Curzon Street) Act prohibited him from taking his line across or beyond the point of junction with the London & Birmingham, and he was not allowed to cross L&B land, except by arches, which again made a junction impossible.

The result was that the viaduct from Bordesley Junction to a dead end abutting the LNWR main line was built and, as Richard Foster says in his New Street history, the viaduct 'Still strides across Bordesley as a monument to the stupidity of short term power struggles'. Its only regular use was as a siding at the Bordesley end for washing cattle wagons.

ordinary passengers when the Midland also moved to New Street, on 1st July 1854. The Midland gained their own portion of a 'rebuilt' New Street on 8th February 1885 when the 'Midland side' was opened.

Traffic development on the east side of Birmingham was outstripping capacity and it was evident that 'something must be done'. An Act of 1888 therefore gave powers for independent passenger and freight lines between Curzon Street and the LNW main line and between Curzon Street and the 'Grand Junction' at Vauxhall. The Grand Junction route

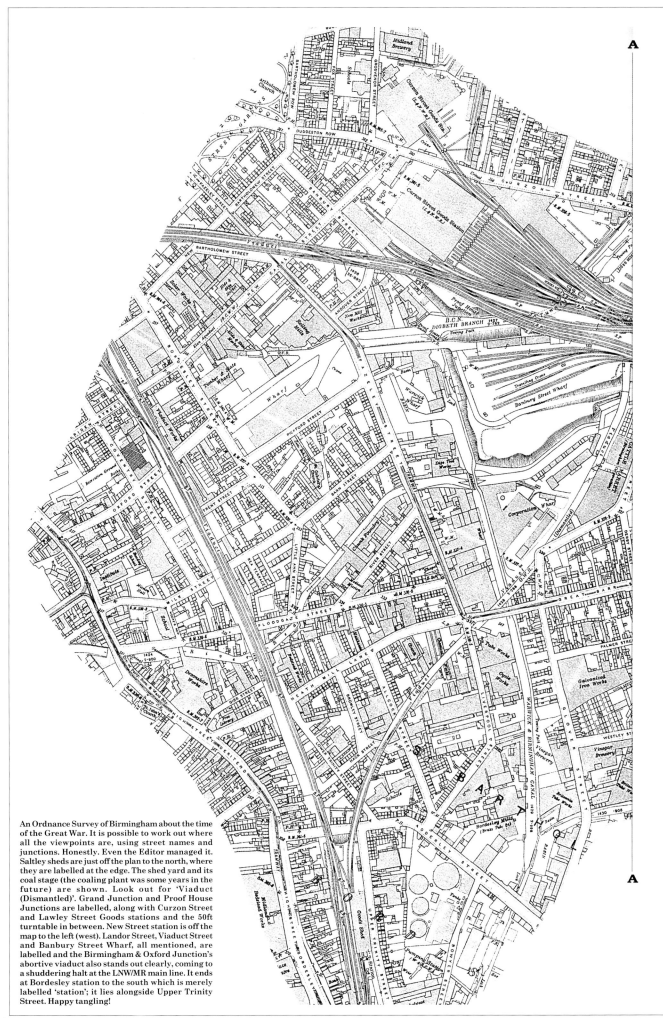

An Ordnance Survey of Birmingham about the time of the Great War. It is possible to work out where all the viewpoints are, using street names and junctions. Honestly. Even the Editor managed it. Saltley sheds are just off the plan to the north, where they are labelled at the edge. The shed yard and its coal stage (the coaling plant was some years in the future) are shown. Look out for 'Viaduct (Dismantled)'. Grand Junction and Proof House Junctions are labelled, along with Curzon Street and Lawley Street Goods stations and the 50ft turntable in between. New Street station is off the map to the left (west). Landor Street, Viaduct Street and Banbury Street Wharf, all mentioned, are labelled and the Birmingham & Oxford Junction's abortive viaduct also stands out clearly, coming to a shuddering halt at the LNW/MR main line. It ends at Bordesley station to the south which is merely labelled 'station'; it lies alongside Upper Trinity Street. Happy tangling!

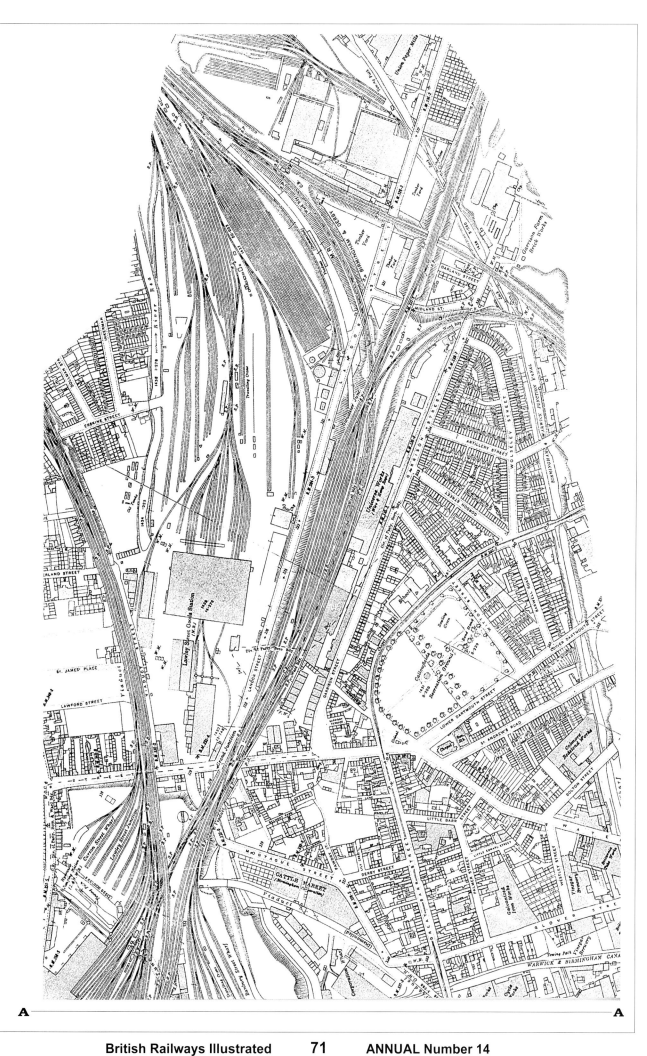

This time, the view is east towards Proof House Junction Box (between gantry and chimney). This was the third 'Proof House' Box and had only been in situ for four months when this view was taken. LNW lines and Curzon Street Depot left, Midland lines right.

The 1893 Aston lines flyover is seen crossing the Up and Down Goods lines and the Curzon Street access lines with Curzon Street No.1 Box prominent. Curzon Street No.2 Box can just be spotted to the right of No.1, where the viaduct descends to the left. The Midland lines are to the right of the picture with Grand Junction Box to the left of the tall signal.

Moving east to Grand Junction we are now looking back towards New Street. To the left is the abortive Birmingham & Oxford Junction viaduct from Bordesley cut off at its interface with the LNW main line but the original intention to get across to Curzon Street is clear. The lines dropping down beneath the viaduct are the Up and Down Goods Lines to Proof House Junction and the Curzon Street access lines to their right. A 'Jinty' waits behind the three armed signal for its turn to cross. Such moves were always a challenge for signalmen to make between main line services.

This is Vauxhall Viaduct. The original routes from Vauxhall to Curzon Street is below and the 1893 'High Level' to Proof House Junction and New Street above. We must be in Birmingham if it's 'Lucas Batteries for Dependability'. A poster on the premises to the right tells us of 'New through Summer services' to somewhere. One brave soul walks along the appropriately named 'Viaduct Street' below whilst LNW arms stand sentry-like above. 'The way we were' indeed.

The wider view of Grand Junction taken from the flyover with Exchange Sidings beyond the Box and Lawley Street Midland Goods below left. The 50ft turntable was seldom used in later years, as the weeds show. Until the 1893 alterations, it was connected to the Grand Junction line at Lawley Street Junction LNW Box. A pleasing collection of signals including an LNW 3-armed backing set up by the viaduct wall. The arms read to Exchange Sidings, Up Camp Hill (Gloucester Line) and Up Derby.

Nearer Grand Junction and looking east. To the right of the box are the Up Gloucester, Up Derby, Down Derby and Down Gloucester lines. On the left are the Up and Down LNW lines to and from Coventry and London. Lawley Street Depot is at the lower level. The 1851-1896 Saltley-Derby Junction curve crossed Landor Street (ahead of us) just this side of the first bridge in the distance, which carries the diverted lines. These then pass under the LNW and emerge as the main lines to the right of Grand Junction Box. Beyond this bridge on Landor Street can be seen a further parapet, advertising a certain brand of bitter. This carries the Midland Saltley-Camp Hill line.

We have reached the 1896 curve from Landor Street Junction (box ahead) where the Midland's Derby-Camp Hill-Kings Norton line went to the right beyond the box which we see the back of. The remains of the 1851 viaduct are to our left and there is considerable activity in Lawley Street Goods Yard beyond. Saltley shed is in the haze in the middle distance with the coaler prominent behind the box.

We are looking towards New Street, through the 'dive under' where the Up and Down Midland lines pass beneath the main LNW Coventry lines and the Up Gloucester line. The remains of the pre-1896 viaduct are on our right.

The 'dead end' of the Birmingham & Oxford Junction's abortive viaduct, never used for a through train. We are alongside the LNW/Midland lines looking towards Bordesley.

The 'wider view' of the viaduct striding towards Bordesley. The sidings in the foreground lead to Banbury Street Wharf.

The northernmost span of the derelict viaduct. The photographer is standing adjacent to the Down Midland line on the New Street side of Proof House Junction. The lane is the access road leading from Montague street to Banbury Street Wharf.

This time we are looking north from the bricked up end of the GW portion. Grand Junction Box is visible to right of centre, above and to the left of that delightful 'Spratts' advert on the end of a building, accompanied by some further gems on the abutments.

Despite the removal of intermediate road bridges, 355 yards of the viaduct remained complete at the Bordesley end with two sidings being available. The only known uses were for 'crippled' wagons awaiting repair and the washing of cattle wagons. The layout did just give a run round from the cattle pens. This is the end of the line, looking in remarkably good condition. At this stage, the track had another 18 years life left.

Looking round the curve from Bordesley North Box, a solitary tank wagon has been abandoned, probably awaiting repairs and in nobody's way in the meantime.

We are now on the viaduct looking towards the Great Western main line. Round the curve to the left is Bordesley station. The wagons to the left are in the cattle pen siding and the 47 lever Bordesley North Box dating from 1918 is above the parapet. The viaduct lines were taken out of use in February 1967.

No tangle at this end, just the simple connection from the viaduct to the sidings at Bordesley North. The wagons are on the cattle pens line and the Up and Down Main and Relief lines towards Snow Hill are to the left of the box. A fine GW signal with route indicator (compare with the LM idea of having three separate arms at Grand Junction) completes our journey from the LNW and Midland Railways to the Great Western by a route never used by a through train.

Grime Time

The steam locomotive was, of course, inherently dirty though it could be kept in perfectly good order, along with the places where it lived. It was only lack of staff and the disinclination to pay them anything worthwhile, together with the obvious fact that all this was going to end pretty soon anyway that saw standards slip so badly. Just how badly can be appreciated in these pictures in which the comprehensive descent into slum conditions at sheds is only too painfully apparent. Poor old 700 class 0-6-0 30316 at Eastleigh recalls the Big Freeze of 1962-63 when a number of 700s were hastily recalled from the dump and fitted with snowploughs. It was February 1963 before the old warrior was

finally got rid of. The two J50 0-6-0Ts, 68970 and 68990 at Hornsey shed (lower left) on 21 February 1960 are testimony enough to the reign of King Neglect while 0-8-0 49070 at Willesden (above) on the same day is not much better. There was a London visit that day obviously, for Mr Idle found himself at Kentish Town too; below, 45514 HOLYHEAD from Millhouses was half respectable but 48142 and 44532 were fairly scruffy. At all the sheds the general clutter and mess on the ground would have had a pre-war Shed Foreman directing culprits to the Labour Exchange. Photographs Paul Hocquard (top left); rest D. Idle. All: The Transport Treasury.

West for Carlisle (and Hawick)

Notes and Photographs by Jim Smith

While Newcastle is best known as the major city on the East Coast main line between London and Edinburgh, it was also the origin of two secondary routes of considerable importance. The first of these served the industrial areas to the south-east of Newcastle, running through Sunderland and Stockton to rejoin the main line at Northallerton. The second – and subject of this article – was the east to west route connecting Newcastle with Carlisle.

Until fairly recently this service operated from the western end of the Central station, utilising platforms 11 to 14, which did not conflict with the main line entering the station by the 90 degree curve leaving the King Edward bridge, although platforms 11 and 12 could be accessed from the bridge. All the traffic at this end of the station was of course directed from the massive signal gantry which spanned the whole width of the layout, operated from signal box No.3 in the 'Y'

between the two routes. The freight lines bypassing the station platforms along the south side divided under the gantry to allow progression either southward over the bridge or westward; in the latter case they had to cross all the lines coming in from the bridge.

Immediately on leaving the station, the Carlisle lines dropped down through the industrial western parts of the city past Elswick (home to major engineering companies including Vickers and

distant viewpoint in Canada that rationalisation of routes around Newcastle has now seen the virtual abandonment of the direct line from the station through Scotswood to Blaydon and that passenger trains now use the former freight line through Dunston to Blaydon. This cross country line was and remains an important alternative route for traffic diverted from either east or west coast main lines for operational reasons. Indeed it is the only east-west route of any capacity between York and Edinburgh.

When I first started observing this line, the through passenger trains were handled by D49 4-4-0s from Carlisle Canal and Blaydon, but these were soon to be replaced by the ubiquitous B1s from Gateshead and Canal. The D49s were transferred away from Canal, although Blaydon retained its two 'Hunts', 62747 THE PERCY and 62771 THE RUFFORD. Carlisle would occasionally send out one of their four A3s, 60068 SIR VISTO (the last to be converted from A10 to A3), 60079 BAYARDO, 60093 CORONACH or 60095 FLAMINGO. All four of these locomotives remained at Carlisle until their last days and did most of their work slogging up and down the Waverley route.

There were two routes to the west between Scotswood and Wylam, the principal one being that which crossed the River Tyne at Scotswood and on through Blaydon. The second remained on the north side of the river, serving Lemington and North Wylam – passing George Stephenson's birthplace. It then crossed the river on a delicate bowstring bridge to join the former line at West Wylam Junction. Both lines would provide rail access to new generating stations which were built in the early 1950s, at Stella South and Stella North – both drawing their coal by rail from local collieries. I was part of the construction team on the latter, including supervision of the new rail connection to the Lemington line, an overbridge and installation of the standage sidings within the station area. A long time ago and now an ocean away!

Armstrong Whitworth, which constructed many locomotives for the NER and overseas systems) to Scotswood, crossed the river to Blaydon and thereafter traversed open country, encountering only small rural towns such as Hexham and Haltwhistle until reaching Carlisle. The total distance is some 60 miles and there are no significant gradients of operational difficulty, although the westerly approach to the Central station sometimes caused a problem for freight or empty-stock trains from Scotswood when they had been stopped to await an opportunity to cross the main lines sweeping in from the bridge.

Passenger traffic between the two cities was – from an indistinct memory – probably a two hour interval service, with a variable commuter service between Newcastle and Hexham. The line was also traversed as far as Border Counties Junction, west of Hexham, by the infrequent trains to and from Hawick. I understand from my

In the summer of 1956 Standard 2-6-0 77011 of Blaydon shed sets out from Newcastle Central Platform 13 with the Saturday afternoon train for Hawick via Hexham and the Border Counties line, passing under the northerly end of the great signal gantry. The engine from this service was most likely to stop over at Hawick until the return service on Monday, there being no weekend traffic over the line.

J39 0-6-0 64871 heaves a string of empty cattle trucks up the grade past No.3 signal box, after being stopped awaiting a path across the main line and through the freight lines behind the station, 28 April 1956. Freight to and from the Carlisle line was something of an unknown quantity to observers at Central Station, as much of it utilised the south-west cut-off from Blaydon through Dunston to Low Fell, where southbound connection was made with the East Coast main line. At Dunston a further junction allowed eastward movement toward King Edward Bridge junction, then past Gateshead shed to connect with the coastal route for Sunderland and Middlesbrough. In this way much of the freight traffic to and from the west never traversed the 'choke point' at Newcastle Central.

On a brilliant summer's evening in July 1951 J25 0-6-0 65667 pulls off the main line to allow a Newcastle bound express to pass shortly afterwards. In the background will rise the massive bulk of Stella South Power Station and Stella North will join it across the river, just this side of the pit heap seen on the horizon. I have the location noted as Peth Lane Box – controlling a level crossing – west of Blaydon.

A little later in the same evening in July 1951 that saw 65667 pulling off the main line, G5 0-4-4T 67268 gleams in the setting sun as she heads for Hexham with a stopping train. This loco was sub-shedded from Blaydon at Hexham and her sparkling condition reflects a great deal of local pride at the country shed. Blaydon with its sub-sheds at Alston, Hexham and Reedsmouth provided most of the motive power for local passenger and freight services to the west of Newcastle; it stood between the A695 from Newcastle and the Carlisle line to the east of Blaydon town. In addition to the two 'Hunts' previously mentioned, it had a mixed allocation of J21, J25 and J39 0-6-0s, Q6 0-8-0s, K1 2-6-0s, J72 and J94 0-6-0Ts for freight work plus several G5 0-4-4Ts and V1/V3 2-6-2Ts for local passenger and empty stock work. The occasional D20 4-4-0 was also on hand from time to time.

G5 0-4-4T 67325 heads the 9.15 North Wylam to Newcastle stopping train past Lemington colliery on 7 February 1953. This is the line on the north bank of the river, providing access to the new Stella North Power Station and in later years was retained only for that purpose after the passenger service had been withdrawn. I wonder, now that the power station has been decommissioned, whether the line has not been lifted altogether. In the background is another feature which has vanished in this diesel and electric age. A rope hauled trolley climbs to the crest of the pit heap to discharge another load of colliery waste, while several figures can be seen scavenging for useable coal which has escaped the screens.

Blaydon roundhouse on a December Sunday in 1951 with D49 4-4-0 62747, J21 0-6-0 65090, G5 0-4-4Ts 67259 and 67316, plus an unidentified Q6 without tender. The 1954 strength was some 70 locos – Gateshead had an allocation of about 95 so it was a respectable shed in strength if not in condition; its two roundhouses had 50ft turntables and an antiquated manual coaling stage.

Blaydon's own N10 0-6-2T, 69095, pauses at the shed access road on 23 December 1951. The Carlisle line is beyond the building seen over the top of the boiler. A feature at Blaydon was the loco off the Saturday afternoon arrival from Hawick; it had no further duties until Monday morning and was often found out of steam – an Edinburgh D49 or D30 perhaps – on the siding alongside the A695.

At West Wylam Junction, nine miles west of Newcastle, two routes north and south of the River Tyne conjoined. A Carlisle express is headed into the junction by Gateshead B1 61011 WATERBUCK, a regular performer on this service. To the left is the delicate bowstring girder bridge carrying the line to North Wylam and Scotswood. I believe that by this time – 29 May 1954 – a weight restriction had been placed on the bridge and heavier locos, including the B1s, were not allowed over it. The turnouts and sidings to the front of the engine serviced a colliery behind the camera.

One of the infrequent appearances of a Canal A3; on 29 May 1954 60095 FLAMINGO approaches the junction from the west at the head of four coaches for Newcastle. The four Pacifics at Carlisle led a very different existence from the rest of their brethren and would rarely be seen south of Newcastle. In later years, when the shed was transferred to the London Midland Region, those A3s which remained on the Canal strength famously never received smoke deflectors.

The afternoon train for Hawick has unusual power in the form of rebuilt D20 62349, which I think has the shed code for Heaton, 52B. This train was usually headed by the engine off the incoming morning service, either from Hawick or Edinburgh, so a failure is assumed to have occurred. The D20s were not regular performers on this line. Gresley updated this one engine of the class with larger, long-travel valves in 1936 with adverse affects on its appearance. Subsequent rebuilds were made by Edward Thompson but without the revised footplating of the earlier example.

Blaydon Q6 0-8-0 63390 heads westwards through the junction with a coke train on 13 September 1958. The string includes a number of the ex-NER high-sided wooden 21T wagons. I assume this was coke intended for the blast furnaces of Barrow, transferred from the previous route over Stainmore, which was now in decline.

With the introduction of DMUs the West Wylam bridge could again accept passenger trains – here a Hexham stopper is coming off the bridge. The lack of exhaust allows a clearer view of the junction.

A trackside view of Gateshead B1 61222 heading into the junction at milepost 9 with seven coaches for Carlisle, 13 September 1958.

At Mickley, the line runs alongside the River Tyne, a sylvan stream in a rural setting before it meets the industrial sprawl of Tyneside. On 9 July 1955, a fine Saturday afternoon, the fireman checks the blowdown as V3 2-6-2T 67656 of Blaydon storms past with a Hexham stopper. Trusty Ford Consul parked on the road opposite – I think we were out of sight of any rail personnel and hopped across the lines to our viewpoint 'up sun'.

One of Blaydon's K1s, 62027, is running well with a westbound fitted freight – keeping ahead of a Carlisle express which followed shortly afterward.

The afternoon stopping train for Hawick headed by 4MT 2-6-0 76024, allocated to Blaydon.

A slight diversion was made up the Border Counties line on 17 July 1955, to witness a 'Ramblers Special' near Deadwater in charge of 4MT 76049 with eight coaches in tow. The wild and beautiful west Cheviot hills offered meagre business for a railway and this must have been the largest load by a long way over this fascinating but doomed route.

Right. Mickley proved to be the furthest west of our 'local' outings along the Carlisle route – the distance and time available did not permit any worthwhile period by the lineside. However we did make two expeditions over the whole route by train in order to experience the action on the west side of the country even though it was dominated by the 'inferior' – in our youthful opinion – London Midland Region. The first was on 6 August 1951; the journey was undistinguished, behind a Gateshead B1 and though we 'did' the three sheds, Canal, Kingmoor and Upperby (presumably by city buses) the main intent was to see and record the last of the D31 4-4-0s reported as being stored at Carlisle Canal, prior to scrapping. In this we succeeded, coming across 62281 on the 'dead' line at Canal shed, complete with sacking over her chimney. She and a few other survivors of her class had recently been renumbered out of the 62000 series to make room for the newly constructed K1 2-6-0s and her cab side shows evidence of some confusion, while the tender bears both NE and British Railways. So she awaited her fate after long and faithful service on the Waverley line.

Below. I'm not sure why we went to Carlisle the second time and although we spent some hours at Citadel station saw none of the activity at the north end, where the Waverley route services originated – the carelessness of youth! This second visit was made on 12 April 1952; the weather was distinctly better than August 1951, but from my records we only left Citadel station to visit Upperby, and even then did not get round the shed. That we spent most of our available time at the south end of the station (not even looking for activity on the Waverley line services at the north end) was nothing short of unbelievable but Coronation Pacific 46223 PRINCESS ALICE looming massively into view with a down express was some compensation.

Bottom right. Coronation Pacific 46246 CITY OF MANCHESTER eases out of the station on 12 April 1952 with a southbound express, past the obviously disused signal box. While these large locomotives were very impressive and powerful – in my opinion they lacked the elegance and beauty of the East Coast Pacifics.

Class 2P 40448 has a good head of steam as she awaits departure with a southbound stopping train, while an unidentified class 5 is similarly impatient on the main up line. Two young spotters are absorbed in their ABCs sitting on a luggage trolley, while waiting for further excitement.

This took the form of compound 40902 hauling a mixed bag of empty stock.

Rebuilt 'Royal Scot' 46109 ROYAL ENGINEER rolls the down 'Thames Clyde Express' into the station – a Holbeck engine in good external condition, it makes an elegant picture with an immaculate train.

One of the named J36 0-6-0s, 65216 BYNG, trundles past Upperby shed with a transfer freight in the late afternoon, against a backdrop of vigorous outpourings from the numerous LMR inhabitants. Thereafter, Carlisle was not on my agenda and I never revisited the route after 1955, preferring to concentrate on the East Coast when time permitted.

Endpiece

A 9F 2-10-0 gets its celebrations in early the night before bonfire night, 1967. Moving off light in the shed yard at Normanton, 92094 was obviously not finding this sort of thing as easy as it used to... Photograph Adrian Booth.